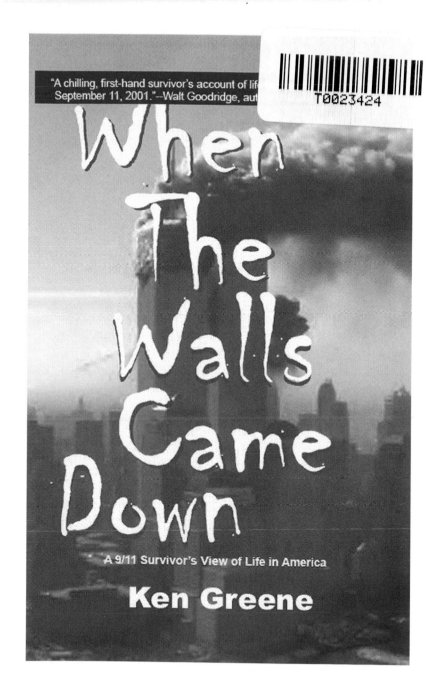

"A chilling, first-hand survivor's account of life
September 11, 2001."--Walt Goodridge, aut

When The Walls Came Down

A 9/11 Survivor's View of Life in America

Ken Greene

When The Walls Came Down
A 9/11 Survivor's View Of Life In America

Copyright © Ken Greene

Published and distributed by
The Passion Profit Company, an imprint of a company called W
email: orderdept@passionprofit.com

© Cover photograph: Maxho.com

Educational institutions, government agencies, libraries and corporations are invited to inquire about quantity discounts.

Retail Cost: $16.95
ISBN-10: 0-9745313-6-7 ISBN-13: 978-0-9745313-6-6
Printed in the United States of America

Library of Congress Cataloging-in-Publication Data

Greene, Ken, 1959-
  When the walls came down : a 9/11 survivor's view of life in America / Ken Greene.
      p. cm.
  Includes bibliographical references and index.
  ISBN 0-9745313-6-7 (alk. paper)
  1. Greene, Ken, 1959- 2. September 11 Terrorist Attacks, 2001--Personal narratives. 3. Port Authority of New York and New Jersey--Officials and employees--Biography. 4. Racism--United States. 5. War on Terrorism, 2001- 6. United States--Race relations. 7. United States--Politics and government--2001- I. Title.
  HV6432.7.G74 2004
  973.931--dc22
  2004018406

Table of Contents

INTRODUCTION

I am one of the fortunate survivors of the September 11, 2001 terrorist attack on the World Trade Center. I was a manager at the Port Authority of New York and New Jersey, and I happened to be in my office in the north tower when the attack occurred.

Like the thousands of others who survived my story will be with me forever. I assisted in the evacuation of the north tower, which was the second tower to fall during the attack. Unlike many other people I am one of the lucky few individuals who crawled out of the north tower after the adjacent south tower fell, and in the process devoured the base of the tower where I was standing.

I barely escaped the north tower before it collapsed.

I waited a little more than two years before writing this book. My intent was always to write it, and waiting a couple of years provided me with enough time and distance from the events of 9/11 to be able to write clearly. It also gave me an opportunity to observe what life in America would be like in the post 9/11 world.

My principal motivation for this book is the continued contradiction between the themes of unity and patriotism in this country since the attack on 9/11, and the reality of the 'business as usual' aspects of everyday life in America. By 'business as usual' I mean the continued discrimination and racism that is perpetuated by too many Americans in the post 9/11 world, as well as the lack of honesty and integrity that is exhibited by many of our government leaders.

The September 11th attack created an environment of self-examination specific to how we live our lives, and how we relate to the world around us, on both an individual and collective basis. Unfortunately, from my perspective, while much has changed at the core *nothing* has changed. At a time when we need to be united as a country in order to effectively deal with issues like terrorism, and social and economic challenges, many of us choose to remain divided by the same old pillars of ignorance.

Since 9/11 I have seen the best and worst of this country. For the most part Americans responded with compassion and empathy for the thousands of individuals and families that were directly affected by the attack. However, after 9/11 the very racism that is endemic to this society in many ways found its way into the forefront.

In particular, people of Middle Eastern decent were collectively branded as suspects and potential terrorists. The hostility they experienced and continue to experience is strong and driven by fear, anger and what some folks would call patriotism.

It is clear to me that we still live with a racial and ethnic divide in America. Part of the reason for this divide is rooted in two distinct versions of history that are taught in this country. The majority of Americans are descendents of the original settlers and immigrants who have experienced America as the land of opportunity. Others of us have had ancestors who had to struggle in order to achieve basic human rights in this country.

Most Americans learn, believe and perpetuate the version of history that is taught in our education system, a version that is espoused as something to be proud of. And for the most part they have bought into a romanticized version of history that is very easy for them to swallow. Others of us look at American history through the eyes of our ancestors, which for blacks and Native Americans in particular is not a history that we would view with such high regard. The near destruction of the Native American civilization and ensuing enslavement of Africans certainly is not a history that I would feel good about.

There are also folks who believe that all of this history is simply 'in the past' or, as I was once told, 'over rated'. Too many of us live with the illusion that all is well in this country. They really believe that we are all harmoniously united with no issues of race, religion, economic class or any of the other categories that have historically created walls between people.

But some of us know better because we see and experience racism, ranging from subtle to overt, just about every day of our lives. Consequently, it continues to be a struggle to reach the point where race is no longer an issue in America.

I want to be clear that I do not believe that discrimination and racism are the *entire* reason for the plights of many people in this country. I believe that it is all too often used as an excuse for the failure to progress socially, educationally and economically. For my fellow black Americans and other ethnic minorities in this country the opportunity to get a good education, start a business or secure a rewarding job or career, and enjoy economic success is significantly better than it was for the generations that have preceded us. We owe it to ourselves to take advantage of each and every opportunity that is available to us, and demand opportunity when and where it is denied to us.

However, this reality does not excuse the behaviors of a large segment of this society.

We are Americans. We profess this country to be the land of freedom, equality, and goodwill toward all men. We claim that we would never intentionally bring harm to innocent people, or deny them their freedoms or destroy their lives. In America we are all equal. Everyone is innocent until proven guilty, etc., etc., etc.

Unfortunately, this belief is not everyone's reality.

Instead of dealing with these issues in a constructive manner, many Americans are quick to jump to the moral high ground based on principles rooted in the revisionist version of good ole' American history. They chose to retreat to the old refrain 'America is the greatest country in the world', as if Americans are the only folks on the globe who think that their country is the absolute best. And as a consequence of their self-righteous attitudes they become barriers to the social progress that is still needed in this country.

I understand that in this day and age whenever issues of race, discrimination, or prejudice are raised a lot of people still get very uncomfortable. In their minds we're not supposed to discuss it. They believe that we should simply see it as a subject whose relevance is long past.

In addition, I know that as a black person when you raise the subject in some circles it is assumed that you are a militant. You are very quickly labeled as an anti-establishment, anti-American militant who is simply looking to provoke people into a confrontation. This is often a very unfair and inaccurate categorization of someone who simply speaks to the subject. I have had frank and meaningful discussions with my friends, both black and white, over the years, and I have not lost a friendship that I can remember because of our discussions. In fact we probably learned a few things about the world and each other in the process.

I fully recognize that race relations in this country have improved over time, and that there are people in this society who do not exhibit the attitudes and behaviors I take issue with. For these folks, treating all people with respect is fundamental to their way of life. In an ideal world, *they* would be representative of every American across the board.

Ironically, one of the aspects of September 11, 2001 that I will always remember is that for one snapshot in time race *didn't* seem to matter. We were simply people who were doing everything that we could to assist one another through an unimaginable crisis. What the world saw was emergency workers helping to save lives, and rescuing people who were in danger. There were thousands of

7

individuals who didn't know each other offering assistance and encouragement throughout the day and immediately thereafter. The 9/11 timeframe was a snapshot of what his country professes to represent on a normal day, and during the following months our collective sentiments seemed to be consistent with that theme.

However, since that time frame, much of America has regressed back to the pre-9/11 world.

Not all Americans. Just *too many* Americans.

And as for the majority of Americans I ask myself what the difference is in their attitudes, politics, and behavior in the post 9/11 world. Honestly, there is *no* difference. They just continue to live comfortably among the many hypocritical Americans who say one thing on race and politics while they practice or support another.

Like all Americans the shock and dismay after the attack on 9/11 was overwhelming, and the event will last with me forever. It was a despicable act that it is still hard to grasp.

Tragically, the walls of the World Trade Center came down that day. Unfortunately, many of the walls that need to come down in this society have proven to be much harder to destroy.

The time for these walls to disappear is long past.

When will they come down?

PART I

SEPTEMBER 11, 2001

Chapter 1

5:00 A.M. Alarm Clock

On September 11, 2001 my wife Gina and I were living in Fairfield, Connecticut, which is approximately fifty miles north of New York City. The alarm clock rang at 5 o'clock that morning, my normal workday wake-up time. As always I eased out of bed as delicately as possible, not wanting to disturb Gina, the world's lightest sleeper. I have to admit that I was rarely successful in my attempts to do so, and that morning was no different.

After whispering good morning in her ear I tiptoed in the dark to the bathroom, and then I took a shower and went through the usual morning ritual. When I finished I tiptoed into the guest room to dress for work. I always watched the local news while getting dressed, and I was looking forward to the fact that the weather forecast called for a warm and sunny day.

9

My routine was measured down to the minute as a result of day-to-day repetition. The walk to the train station was precisely twelve minutes long during good weather days and walking conditions, twelve to fourteen minutes in the rain or snow to accommodate puddles along the way, and fifteen to eighteen minutes if there was ice on the ground after a snowfall. I factored in a four-minute early arrival time at the station in the event that the 6:08 a.m. commuter train to Manhattan was running ahead of schedule.

The train, which is the main commuter line servicing Connecticut, originated in the city of New Haven and worked its way south along the Long Island Sound. It traveled through lower New Haven County into several of the affluent bedroom towns that comprise Fairfield County, otherwise known as the 'Gold Coast of Connecticut'. From there it continued through Westchester County, New York and down to Manhattan.

I found myself running approximately three minutes late in my routine that morning, and quickly headed for the front door without fully buttoning my shirt and fixing my tie. Gina was already out of bed and standing in the vestibule by the front door.

"Honey, I'll lock the door when you leave. Give me a call later when you know the train that you're going to catch tonight," she said. Gina was headed to the city later that morning and planned to meet me for the return trip home. She locked the door behind me as I hurried off to the station on my way to the World Trade Center.

As I headed to the station a thought crossed my mind. I had failed to kiss her good-bye that morning, which was the most important part of my morning ritual. I could not remember the last time that I had failed to do so. But it was clearly an oversight that I couldn't correct that morning without missing my train. And besides, in my mind she would understand. I could always apologize when I got home, and continue the practice the next day. September

11th would be like any other day, and I was sure that I would be getting out of bed to go to work for years to come anyway. At the age of forty-two I had a long time left in the work world, and I would just make sure to kiss her twice the following morning. That was the plan.

So I thought.

Gina had and continues to have her own business working out of her home-based office. She provides consulting services to not-for-profit foundations in the areas of marketing and communications. Unlike my near two-hour one-way commute to the World Trade Center her commute to the office was approximately ten seconds. However, she typically began her day shortly after I left for the train and was often still working when I got home.

I have to admit that on occasion I fumed about the imbalance in our respective commuting times, especially when there were train delays or cancellations. However, the best thing for me to do was to suffer in silence.

Back in 1997, I was working for Supervalu, Inc., a Fortune 100 company in the grocery retail and distribution industry. We relocated from Minneapolis, Minnesota to Pittsburgh, Pennsylvania in a job-related move for me. While home shopping in Pittsburgh, I was emphatic that we should find a location where the average commuting time for each of us was no more than one hour. In my mind a total of up to two hours between the two of us seemed perfectly reasonable. Gina didn't necessarily see it that way, but after some debate she ultimately went along with my brilliant theory.

During the year 2000, I accepted a position with a Connecticut based 'dot-com' company that was also in the grocery industry, and Fairfield was a town that I was familiar with. It was perfectly situated. Gina could work from home and my commute was only eight miles up the highway. Unfortunately, the 'dot-com' venture lasted only five months.

My next opportunity was with the Port Authority of New York and New Jersey, whose corporate offices were based in the World Trade Center. I had worked for the agency from 1981 through 1995, and decided to take advantage of an opportunity to return.

Shortly after re-joining the Port Authority I hinted at the imbalance in our commute times, and was reminded about my 'average of an hour each' theory. Gina said, "You know, our total one-way commuting time is less than two hours. If you remember, I wasn't sold on your idea but you were adamant that it made sense. Well?"

What could I say? She was correct. My one-way commute was an hour and forty-five minutes and she commuted for fifteen seconds at the most.

So much for my commuting time logic!

6:08 a.m. - Train to Manhattan

The 6:08 train pulled into Fairfield on time. I took my jacket off, and put it on the overhead rack and sat in a seat by the window. As always, I was certain that a predictable aspect of my morning commute would take place.

I was one of the few black commuters on the train, and the white commuters would almost always *avoid* sitting next to me unless there were no other seats available in the car. There were mornings when I would sit by myself during the entire trip to Grand Central Terminal in midtown Manhattan. Even though I was neatly dressed in a business suit and tie, and carrying a briefcase like everyone else, something about me was clearly uncomfortable for my fellow commuters. The only difference that I could determine was the color of my skin.

After surveying the car, and in many cases walking to the car either in front or in back of me, some of the men would resign themselves to sitting next to me. The usual approach was to put their briefcase on the floor or on the

12

overhead rack, and sit down and stare straight ahead or read a newspaper opened just wide enough to ensure that there could be no eye contact between us. They would do whatever was necessary to avoid eye contact. I always said good morning, because it was the friendly, neighborly fellow-American thing to do.

A high-end response was normally a grunt at best. However, the more typical response was absolutely no recognition that I had uttered a word.

But I have to admit that the men weren't nearly as bad as the women.

The women were even more uncomfortable sitting next to me. Many would prefer to stand station after station until a seat became available somewhere else. Sometimes they would stand directly in front of me. I supposed that they feared being harassed, propositioned, or maybe even mugged. Imagine that. Being mugged on a crowded commuter train in full view of dozens of hostile commuters as the train moved along. Clearly, I was someone to fear. Maybe they thought I would grab their handbag, kick out the window, and leap onto the tracks while we were moving at sixty miles an hour. Makes sense to me.

I have to admit that the dynamics of my commute to New York were not the least bit surprising. I commuted from Edison, New Jersey to the World Trade Center in the early 1990's and the dynamics were precisely the same. Being black has been a life long affliction when riding the commuter lines in the allegedly cosmopolitan, highly sophisticated New York City metropolitan area.

Admittedly, there was a time in my life when my experiences on the train would have bothered me, but as I have grown older I have learned to recognize how things *really* are in too much of this country. I have chosen to do what I need to do in order for me to be happy and successful *in spite* of the some of the people around me.

13

And when I think about it, who was the disaffected party on the train? Was it me, who made myself comfortable in a seat that I paid for, or my fellow commuter who also paid for a seat but chose to stand for an hour? I would simply put my headphones on and listen to music and gaze in their direction in amazement every now and then as they stood by the door tired after a long workday.

I once heard a joke that the only thing more threatening to some white folks than a black man with a gun in his hand is a black man in a business suit with a briefcase and a college degree. My life long observations have validated this 'joke' as having merit. Back in grade school we were all taught the 'all men are created equal' version of good ole' American folklore. I guess that exclusions to that rule include 'commuting while black'.

We are all familiar with the 'driving while black' phenomena, which occurs when a black motorist is pulled over by a police officer for no other reason than being black, and often times questioned about driving in a certain community or made to prove that we own the vehicle that we're driving. Sometimes we're searched and/or detained for no apparent reason.

I have had that experience on at least five occasions and never received so much as a warning from a police officer! I was simply driving a Nissan 280ZX sports car, which was a warning sign to some people that given my race either an auto theft had occurred or a drug dealer was in the vicinity.

When I think about it I suppose that I can't complain. I have never been pulled off of a train and held by police officers for 'commuting while black'. Not yet. I guess that 'CWB' can be *offensive* without being an offense.

No Room At The Inn

Unfortunately, the commuting phenomenon was not inconsistent with other experiences living in Fairfield.

In July 2001, just *two* months before 9/11, Gina began the process of finding an assisted living community for her mother who is in her eighties and required help with managing her day-to-day affairs. Her mother lived in an apartment in Westchester County for thirty-four years, and was and continues to be very independent. However, the effects of the aging process and a recent hospitalization for a heart condition made it very difficult for her to fully function on her own.

Gina and I felt that it would be best to find an assisted living community in the town of Fairfield. Like many other families facing the same situation we wanted her to live near us, and to be confident that she was in a high quality facility that would meet her needs. Terry, Gina's only sibling and older brother, happened to live quite a distance away in Alabama.

We also felt that keeping their mother in the region that she had lived in all of her life was the most logical approach to take. This wasn't an unreasonable desire. Children of the elderly make these kinds of decisions all of the time.

Gina called an assisted living facility in town to get information about their program. She spoke with the head administrator and told him that we lived in Fairfield and wanted to find a good place for her mother to live. The administrator was all too happy to tell her about the living options and amenities available to the residents, and invited her to come in for a visit.

"Your mother would enjoy it here" he told her, "We have very good programs for seniors. The nurses and support staff are always available to assist the residents. Once she gets situated she will be able to make friends in the community. You'll be satisfied that you made a good decision." He also *assured* Gina that there were units available if her mother needed to move in quickly. It could be arranged with no problem. "Let's schedule an appointment for you to come in and visit with us. I can't wait to meet you."

Gina stopped by the facility to pick up an application on the way home from her exercise class at the local YMCA. When she arrived she was greeted by a receptionist who provided her with an application package. She took it home and filled it out, and called for additional information and to schedule an appointment to see the facility.

When she reached the administrator the story changed entirely. "Um, Miss Toppins" he nervously stumbled, "um, there was a mistake with the information that I gave you. Unfortunately, there are, um, no units available at this time. Apparently, we, we um, had committed them before this appointment. I'm sorry. We will let you know if things should change." There was no friendly chitchat, no invitation extended to tour the facility and no follow-up information. And there wasn't any discussion about putting her name on a waiting list.

Isn't it strange how the situation immediately went from having *several* units still open to having *nothing* available in the same day! There was no room in the inn! The very same administrator who handled the enrollment process was in error about having *several* units available!

Let me guess what went on here. It couldn't have been the fact that a black woman walked into the facility. It was the year 2001.

This is America – that couldn't possibly have been it.

Besides, I personally know that black women were welcome in the facility. I had seen them with my own eyes enter and exit the facility as I walked home from the train station. They cook meals, clean floors, change bedpans and iron clothes. I'm sure that they also make wonderful nurses

16

and aides. I bet that the residents just love having them around to meet their needs.

But live there? Now that was another story – the message was clear: *no room at the inn for a black person unless they are wearing an apron or a nurse's uniform.*

Maybe Gina should have told the administrator that we were one of the black families that snuck into town under the cover of darkness before scheduling an appointment.

As it turned out we found an assisted living facility in Westchester County that was better suited to her mother's needs. She is able to socialize comfortably with her fellow residents, and she is unlikely to have a visitor ask her to take out the trash or fix their parent a meal if they should see her in the hallway.

Chapter 2

7:20 A.M. - Grand Central Terminal to the World Trade Center

The train made its way down the coast through Greenwich, Connecticut; Westchester County and then continued through the Bronx on its way to Manhattan. As we passed by the Kingsbridge Station in the Bronx I was whisked back to my childhood growing up in that neighborhood. Being a kid from the Bronx was a great experience for me. If I had to do it all over again I would chose the same neighborhood, same friends and same schools.

When we finally reached Grand Central Terminal it was the usual scene. During the morning and afternoon rush hours it is an incredible maze of commuters walking a mile a minute in seemingly every direction. The place is all business. The world's busiest train terminal, used by an estimated seven hundred thousand people on a daily basis, was fully alive as the New York region began the workday.

I got off of the train and walked briskly across the main concourse headed to the subway, and I rode the escalators down to the hot and crowded platform on the sub-grade level of the terminal along with a sea of commuters headed downtown. Although the subway trains typically ran two or three minutes apart the wait on the platform always seemed to take much longer, especially on those warm mornings when the hot stale air just sat in the station. We were all pushed together, typically jockeying for a spot on the platform where the doors opened. This was all a part of the commuting game. Having grown up in the city and ridden subways most of my life, I considered myself an expert in the art of 'platform jockeying'.

I didn't have the usual success that particular morning. The line was three deep when the first train entered the station. The second train was equally as crowded, and after a few dozen people pushed their way off, a few of us pushed our way on.

It was just another day in paradise.

The ride south to the Fulton Street Station was shoulder to shoulder, and as always I was more than happy to get off of the train when we arrived. The World Trade Center was only one block from Fulton Street, and I took my time and enjoyed the little bit of gorgeous weather that I thought that I would be able to take advantage of that day.

I crossed Church Street and walked across the World Trade Center plaza. It was one of my favorite places in the city. The plaza was a wide-open space, with a circular black marble fountain in the center surrounded by concrete benches to sit on and enjoy the weather and people watch on a nice day. During the warm weather months free midday concerts were performed on the plaza. It was a very popular gathering place.

I loved working at the World Trade Center, which was built by the Port Authority and opened in the early 1970's. The complex was the agency's flagship, and our employees took a great pride in working there. The entire world knew where the World Trade Center was, and what it represented to New York and the country. It was the international symbol of American commerce.

Whenever anyone asked where I worked I simply replied, "The World Trade Center". There were never any additional details required.

For me it was the most unique place on the planet, and much more than the two one hundred and ten story towers. The concourse level of the complex had a terrific mix of retail stores. Hundreds of tourists could be found walking around the concourse shopping, or simply marveling at the incredible design of the complex. An estimated one hundred and forty thousand people visited the World Trade Center on an average day.

The concourse level entrance of the north tower where I worked faced West Street and was connected to the World Financial Center. It was just across the street from Battery Park City, a beautiful high-rise development with a park, boat marina, and scenic walkway along the Hudson River.

Windows on the World was the restaurant at the top of the north tower. The Observation Deck was atop the south tower. Both offered an incredible view of the region.

Workers as well as tourists also enjoyed being outside on the plaza level, which was the level immediately above the concourse facing east. Sun up to sun down cameras snapped pictures of the towers and their incredible surroundings. I cannot remember how many times I was asked by a tourist to take a picture of them standing in front of one of the towers. I often took pictures while I was in a squatting position, looking up at them in an attempt to capture the entire height of one of the towers in the background.

After a while some of us who worked at the World Trade Center probably took for granted how unique the complex was. When you work at a particular location for a long period of time the environment can wear off on you. However, the relationship that we all had with the towers was one that you would have had to have worked there to understand. When we were within the four borders of the complex it was a different world.

The World Trade Center had an energy and vibrancy you could feel every day of the week. Approximately fifty thousand people worked in the complex, enough people to fill Yankee Stadium. And there were over four hundred businesses from close to thirty countries that had offices in the complex. It was a mini-international city unto itself.

Gina and I had been away from the New York area for five and a half years, and although I had lived in other parts of the country my re-engagement with the World Trade Center environment was immediate. I had a new appreciation for how truly special a place it was.

But beyond working there it held a much more *important* significance.

The World Trade Center is where I met Gina, who is also a former Port Authority employee. She was a manager in the aviation department when I was working in our general services department during my first stint with the agency. Although I met Gina in 1981 we did not become close friends until 1992. We used to meet for lunch on the plaza during the warm weather months. The plaza was where I asked her for our first date. We went to a New York Jets football game, and it took me about a week to get up the nerve to ask her to go with me.

We eventually got engaged in 1993 and were married on New Year's Day in 1994. Gina and I purchased our wedding bands from the W. Kodak jewelry store that was located on the concourse of the World Trade Center.

We are not an unusual couple by Port Authority standards. There are several current and former employees who met and married while working for the agency.

I was initially hired by the agency when I graduated from college at the end of 1980. I spent fifteen years there before relocating to Minneapolis, and worked with some very good people during those years. However, my return in May 2001 lasted for a period of one year. Given my time away working in the private sector for a Fortune 100 company, and subsequently for an entrepreneurial start-up business, the processes and constraints of the government

21

made for a very difficult transition. I knew at some point the private sector would be the best long term fit for me.

Career preference not withstanding, I took pride in the work being performed by the Port Authority. The mission of the agency is to provide a high quality service to the commuters and other travelers who use the tunnels and bridges that connect New York and New Jersey, as well as the airports and bus terminals in the region in order to conduct their day-to-day affairs.

The New York region is both tough and demanding, and the responsibility for managing major transportation facilities requires a level of resilience and determination that would be our saving grace as the day unfolded.

7:50 a.m. – The Work Day Begins

I took an express elevator from the concourse to the forty-fourth floor of the north tower, and a local elevator from there to my office on the sixty-fifth floor. I enjoyed working on a floor that high up in the tower in a nice office in the northeast corner. The view was fantastic – I could see the George Washington Bridge to the northwest, midtown Manhattan up to and beyond the Empire State Building, and the East River.

Every morning when I arrived I took my jacket off, put it on the back of my chair, and looked out of the window for a moment taking in the view and thinking about the day ahead. On September 11th the sky was so clear that I could see the frame of the George Washington Bridge, which was approximately twelve miles away. I thought to myself that the day was going to be especially beautiful, and that during my lunch break if I could find some time I would take a walk east to the South Street Seaport.

The second half of the morning routine was a quick trip down to the cafeteria on the forty-third floor. It was time to satisfy my one-cup-of-coffee-a-day fix. The usual group of employees were scattered around the cafeteria, and I was always amazed by the folks who went for the full course breakfast spread: eggs, bacon, toast, orange juice, coffee, etc. I would probably find myself sinking into a lethargic mode after eating that kind of breakfast.

Cup of coffee in hand, it was back to the office to read through my e-mails and start the workday. At that time I was the Assistant Director, Aviation – Operations for the agency, and I was working on a variety of initiatives in support of the operations, maintenance, security, and airfield technology functions for the New York metropolitan area airport system.

The job was quite interesting. The airport system is among the busiest and most complex in the world, and the day-to-day activities associated with being a part of the management team were rewarding. Like any job it had its frustrations but I learned that the best approach was to ensure that I kept an appropriate balance between my professional and personal life.

And on that day I was about to learn something else.

Little did I know that the same person who wasn't 'good enough' for his fellow commuters to sit next to on the train, and whose mother-in-law wasn't 'good enough' to live in a senior citizens environment with their parents, was about to be 'good enough' to find himself helping save the lives of folks like them.

Chapter 3

8:46 A.M. – The North Tower is Hit

Ken

I had just finished reading through my e-mails and some of the administrative work on my desk. Jeanne, a fellow department staff member, had returned to work that day after being out for several days dealing with a family matter. She and I had just begun working together in August, and had become very close colleagues in a short period of time. Jeanne was under a lot of pressure and stress while tending to her family's affairs, and I was very concerned about where the situation stood upon her return. We spoke in her office, which was the second one down from me on the east window line of the tower.

As we were speaking we heard and felt an incredible explosion. The tower actually moved to my right, and then recoiled to the left before steadying. For a fleeting second I had the distinct feeling that it was going to fall over. The explosion moved furniture and file cabinets, and rolled people sideways who were sitting in their chairs.

It was a *major* explosion.

I ran back to my office and looked out of my window, which was facing to the north. Paper and pieces of the building were falling from the sky like confetti; the kind of confetti that fell during those parades up Broadway after the Yankees or Mets won a World Series.

My first thought was that a mechanical equipment room exploded and blew out windows above our floor. But whatever it was, it was forceful enough to move the tower and create a stream of falling debris.

My instinct was to leave the office immediately, but to first check my side of the floor in order to ensure that the employees were evacuating their offices and heading to the emergency stairwells. Everyone was stunned, and some folks actually went back to their offices and sat speechless and confused. But after a minute or two it became clear that the best thing to do was to leave the floor.

After checking my area of the floor to make sure that everyone had vacated there was no time to go back to my office for my jacket or briefcase, or to make a telephone call in an attempt to find out what had happened. I immediately joined my fellow employees in the stairwell and headed to the base of the tower.

The stairwell, which was just wide enough for two people to walk side-by-side comfortably, was full of smoke. Although we were all frightened the crowd did it's best to walk down the steps in as calm and orderly a fashion as possible. There was quite a bit of confusion, and several of us covered our faces with clothing or napkins and newspapers to filter the smoke as much as possible.

The stairwell was very crowded when I entered it. Quite a few people from the floors above us had already been in the process of evacuating the tower, and right away it was very clear that getting to the bottom would be a slow process. It felt at some points like we were standing in a crowded elevator.

As we made our way down the stairs I met up with a World Trade Center operations employee. He had a handheld radio and had received information about what happened as we were walking down the stairs. He said to me, "I was told that a large plane hit the building. I don't believe it." My immediate response was, "Don't repeat this information to anyone else. You need to keep it between us. Some of these folks might freak out if they know what happened. We need to work to keep people moving as quickly as possible." He agreed, and promised to keep what he knew between the two of us.

One hysterical employee two landings above us was screaming, "They tried to get us the last time, and now they are trying again. This time they are going to kill all of us. We told these people that we shouldn't work here but nobody listens. They are going to kill us." Fortunately I knew the employee so I stopped at the base of a landing and waited for him to come down. Then I grabbed his arm and tried to calm him down.

"This wasn't an attack" I said, "it was a bad airplane accident. Let's try to calm down and get out of the tower. We are all on one big team and everybody needs to pull their weight." I told him that, "We will be back in the building tomorrow and I'll buy you lunch." His panic calmed to a mumble. Under the circumstances, if a mumble was the best that I could get I would take it.

My original thought was that the airplane was a small Cessna-type private jet that somehow got lost, or had a pilot that had experienced some sort of medical emergency and lost control. But given the impact of the crash on the tower that we witnessed from the sixty-fifth floor it could not have logically been a small aircraft. And besides, the operations employee told me with a level of certainty that it was a large plane that was involved in the accident.

I wondered what would cause a large airplane to hit the World Trade Center. Something was very strange. It was an exceptionally clear day and the flight paths for a large plane were nowhere near the World Trade Center. In addition, pilots are taught to water land in an emergency, if possible, and the East River and Hudson River and Bay were all in the immediate vicinity.

Regardless, it was clear that we needed to get out of the tower as quickly as possible.

The effort to make our way down the stairs proved to be difficult. As we made our way down in the tower, to my amazement I began to see firemen coming up the stairs at about the thirtieth floor. They were fully equipped in their helmets and coats, and wearing heavy boots and carrying sixty pound oxygen tanks on their backs. I cannot imagine the incredible effort that these folks exerted to get to the people trapped above us in the tower. Walking up thirty plus flights of stairs would be an extremely difficult challenge for the average person without carrying anything. *But in a time of incredible crisis these heroes were doing what they were trained to do, and showed tremendous courage going into undefined danger.*

When we got below the thirtieth floor the process of moving down the stairs slowed down considerably. On every other landing we would all stop walking, and lean against the exterior stairwell wall so that the firefighters had a clear path up one side of the stairwell.

I remember yelling to people above me no less than a dozen times, "Everybody stop and lean against the wall. Firemen are coming your way!" Most of us were calm enough to do so. But others were so frightened and panicked that they continued to forcefully push their way down the stairs, as if they could climb over or slip their way through the crowd.

Not that I could blame them.

My instincts told me that if the crowd continued to start and stop moving we would eventually get trampled by a group that was in a state of panic. But one way or another we had to find our way to the base of the tower, and calm would be our only savior.

Fortunately, at the time we didn't have any clues as to what the future would bring.

Gina

Gina had scheduled a heating oil delivery for early that morning, and was waiting for the deliveryman to arrive before leaving the house for a dental appointment in Manhattan. She had just finished eating her breakfast and was in her office writing e-mails to her clients regarding the status of her projects.

The radio was on and she was listening to the Tom Joyner Show, a nationally syndicated black radio program that had been our favorite morning show since the day it came on in the New York area. Unfortunately, the program was eventually dropped from the station because it was not 'New York centric'. Certainly it couldn't have been the music that was the problem. The station played the same top hits as the other stations on the dial, and covered local sports and provided weather updates just like they did.

But according to the station's management the audience didn't care for a broader perspective of news and entertainment beyond the often insular four walls around New York City.

As a native New Yorker I have always known that for a lot of its residents New York is the only relevant place in the world. In their minds New York is the only place where you can find a good restaurant, see a good play, buy fashionable clothing, attend an exciting sporting event, and have a high level conversation. It is the self-proclaimed 'multi-cultural cosmopolitan capital of intellect and sophistication'.

I don't necessarily see it that way.

As proud as I am of having grown up in New York City, I can truthfully say that some of the most ignorant and bigoted people that I have ever come across live amongst the resident population. Not the majority, but a representative number nonetheless—especially the know-it-all crowd—many of whom have never been outside the five boroughs or even their own neighborhood for that matter.

Given that fact I'm not surprised that a radio program that mixes humor and fun with topics designed to intellectually challenge its listeners to think about national and world events, without being New York centric, wouldn't survive.

The Tom Joyner Show encourages its listeners to vote and become politically proactive. It provides scholarships for youngsters striving for a college education at historically black colleges and universities, and financial support to families in need as a part of its mission. The show engages socially conscious media personalities like Tavis Smiley to talk about race relations and politics in America, and their impact on the minority community.

Apparently, this kind of agenda isn't sophisticated enough for the New York listener base. I guess that what the 'multi-cultural capital of intellect and sophistication' needs is more hip-hop on the radio, more news about which music artists are in trouble, about who wore what to the awards show, who is sleeping with whom and who is having who's baby. You know, real meaningful stuff.

I enjoy hip-hop music quite a bit, and I probably listen to more music than the average person. But I also know that it is important to be knowledgeable about important issues that affect our everyday lives. There are too many people out here who are totally disconnected from the important issues because they immerse themselves in the easy stuff, the feel good stuff.

29

Tom Joyner's show was interrupted by the local news affiliate with a special bulletin regarding an explosion at the World Trade Center. Startled, Gina ran to the television and turned it on to see what was happening. All of the news stations were broadcasting that a large airplane had struck the north tower, and that there was a fire burning in the upper floors. She immediately grabbed the telephone and left a voice mail message for me at my office attempting to tell me that if I had a problem getting home once I got out of the tower I should head to our dentist's office in mid-Manhattan. Then she called the dentist and cancelled her appointment. At the time no one in his office was aware of what had happened at the World Trade Center.

Kristian, my youngest brother who lives and works in the Washington D.C. area, was in his office at the Howard Hughes Institute when he heard the news. He had just stepped out to the cafeteria when he received a voicemail message from my brother-in-law, Kenneth, telling him what happened, and asking him to call my office. Kenneth happened to be at work in the U.S. Dept of Immigration offices on Broadway, just a few blocks from where I was.

Kris called my office and got my voicemail. His message was for me to evacuate the building as soon as possible. Subsequently, he called my brother-in-law back and learned that he was being evacuated and was on his way home to Brooklyn.

Then Kris tried to reach me again with no success.

At that point he called Gina and asked her if she had heard the news, and wanted to know if I went directly to the office that morning or had headed from home to one of the airports. Gina told him that I went straight to the World Trade Center, but that she was not worried about my safety. The plane hit the tower several floors above my office and she had left me a message to leave as quickly as possible. After a short conversation Gina and Kris got off of the telephone and continued to follow the media coverage.

Chapter 4

9:03 A.M. – The South Tower is Hit

Ken

The south tower was struck by the second airplane. Fortunately, those of us in the stairwell had no idea that the other tower had been struck. I firmly believe that if we had been aware of the second plane hitting the south tower mass hysteria would have broken loose.

I estimate that we were probably somewhere between the thirty-fifth and fortieth floors at the time that the south tower was hit. It never occurred to me that we could have been under attack and that war had been declared on our country. In my mind an accident happened and we were in the process of evacuating for safety reasons. I really believed that the firemen would address the situation, and that normalcy would be restored.

By the time we reached the vicinity of the lower floors we had been breathing smoke for at least a half an hour and my eyes were starting to sting. And at that point I found myself beginning to walk through as much as six inches of water in the stairwell. The steps became very slippery, and people were losing their footing and sliding forward while

31

trying to hold onto the railings. By now I had put my tie in my mouth, and had pulled my shirt out of my pants and put it up to my face in an effort to filter the smoke. It was very hard to breathe, and all of us had our noses and mouths covered while we were slipping on the steps.

There was also an increasing number of firefighters working their way up the stairwell, and it took a great deal of focus to lean against the wall to give them a path up the stairs while not falling down.

In a strange way I got the sense that the level of panic was not as great as it had been when we entered the stairwell. Maybe it was because we were closer to the base of the tower and believed that the worst was behind us. We all probably felt that in a few minutes we would be on the plaza and could walk away from the complex and go home.

At one point the smoke cleared up a little bit and I overheard a couple of women joking about having the rest of the day off. "As soon as we get out of here let's go shopping at Century 21 (the department store directly across the street) for new clothes," one of them said, "This morning would be a good time to go shopping. There won't be anyone in the store. No lines. I'll just pick up a few things and go home."

It didn't seem like a bad idea at the time.

Maybe the evacuation experience during the bombing in 1993 prepared us for being in the stairwells in an emergency situation. Although I worked at the World Trade Center at that time I was not in the tower when the bombing occurred. Back in 1993 the stairwells were filled with smoke as well and many of the evacuees were in the dark. This time we never lost lighting, and the steps and railings were equipped with luminescent tape to highlight the stairwells if lighting was lost. To a certain extent we were better prepared to handle the stairwells in an emergency after the 1993 bombing. And besides, the end of the ordeal was near.

So we thought...

Gina

When the south tower fell, Kris immediately called Gina, and she asked him to set up a three-way conference call with my mother. Mom was in Iowa visiting my sister Raquel and my nephew Kellen. At first Kris was reluctant to do so because he did not want to upset my mother. They thought that at the time she was alone in my sister's apartment while Raquel was at work and Kellen was at school. He tried to contact my brother Kyle, who lives in California with his wife Jodi and their twin daughters, without success. Then he attempted to contact my Aunt Kathy and Uncle Hubie in Boston, also without success.

After giving it some thought, they called my mother. She was already aware of what had happened and was watching the coverage on television. Gina felt that my mother was exceptionally calm, and that she had a lot of faith that I would be safe and unharmed by the attack. Raquel, a Russian language professor at Grinnell University, had not yet left for the campus. She was very upset and crying about the news and her fear that I was still somewhere in the tower. My mother attempted to convince her to go to the campus and tried to reassure her that everything would be fine.

Ultimately, Raquel went to the campus, and cancelled her class and went back home.

Like the rest of the world, the only thing that my family could collectively do was helplessly watch the news coverage. They were left with hoping for the best in an unbelievable situation with no clear understanding of what was happening. Thinking back, I cannot imagine the terror that they and the millions of people watching the news coverage must have felt.

Gina and my mother remained on the telephone and watched the television coverage. After a while she began

33

receiving phone calls from friends and family asking about my situation. The only information that she could provide was that I went to the office that morning, and that my floor was located below the fire line. One of the calls was from her close friend Sue, who was supposed to be meeting me after work for dinner in the city. Sue was in tears and could not be comforted by Gina given the lack of information regarding my whereabouts.

By now Kris had exited the phone call and went to watch the television coverage in the institute's conference center, leaving Gina and my mother together on the line.

9:30 A.M. – The North Tower Mezzanine and Plaza

Ken

After a harrowing experience, we finally reached the bottom level of the stairwell, and for a split second I felt a sense of relief. It appeared that the ordeal was about to be over. As we got down to the last few floors my plan was to take the subway up to the Port Authority Bus Terminal in midtown Manhattan and stop by the Manager's Office. I thought that I could get some information about what had happened, and make a few telephone calls to figure out what I should do next. I figured that in all likelihood the aviation management team would have a staff meeting at one of the airports to regroup.

Then I stepped out of the stairwell onto the mezzanine, and I learned that the world had changed forever.

What I witnessed was beyond my wildest imagination. It was disturbing beyond belief, and a scene so distressing that I began to feel physically ill. I actually thought that I was going to throw up on the carpet. The mezzanine windows, which were about two stories high and separated by a series of columns, were stained with blood and debris. And there were fires burning on the plaza.

As I looked out toward the huge black marble fountain, which was facing east to Church Street, I could see that there were dead bodies and body parts scattered on the plaza. The entire scene took on the dimension of a horror movie. In my mind it couldn't have been real - I had to be imagining something that could not have occurred.

There was incredible chaos on the mezzanine as people looked out at the plaza. Many broke down in tears, or screamed as a result of what they witnessed. I cannot remember ever hearing bone-chilling screams on the order of what I heard that day. "Oh my God! What happened out there? There are dead bodies! Stuff burning! What is going on? Please, somebody tell me what is going on!!" In some cases people actually sat down on the carpet, paralyzed with fear and disbelief.

Not that I was entirely calm and composed.

We knew that we were far from safety at that point, and that the next step was to take the escalators from the mezzanine down to the concourse level. Everyone was being directed to make a left at the base of the escalators, run across the enclosed concourse past the stores, and leave the complex through the exits east on Church Street. There were emergency rescue personnel directing people on the concourse to their safety.

There were also police, fire rescue, security personnel and Port Authority management staff on the mezzanine level attempting to direct traffic. Among them was Ernesto Butcher, our chief operating officer, who was doing everything that he could to bring some order to the chaos. I spotted him in the vicinity of the escalators, and I ran over in an attempt to get information about what happened. His concern was for the safety of the people being evacuated down the escalators, as well as the ability of the police and firefighters to walk up the escalators to the mezzanine after entering the tower from the concourse level.

I made an instinctive decision that I wanted to stay in the building and help with the evacuation, and asked him what I could do. He responded, "I need you to supervise the escalators, and make sure that the firemen can get up here while people try to go down." Firemen were attempting to come up the escalators from the concourse and they needed one side to be clear.

My role in the evacuation process was to position myself at the top of the escalators, and direct the flow of traffic up from and down to the concourse. The real challenge was to make sure that everyone used the right side of the escalator bank to walk down to the concourse so that emergency rescue personnel could walk up from the concourse level on the left side.

Admittedly a part of me thought about heading for the escalators and running for my life. However, I knew that we were all in a bad situation and needed folks to manage the chaos, so I ran over to a Port Authority Police Officer who directed me to a stack of hard hats in a box. "You better put one of those on," he said, "It's not safe to stay up here without one."

I exchanged a few short words with a fireman, put a helmet on, and grabbed a security guard to help me before heading back to escalators to direct traffic. I said to him, "We have nothing but chaos over by the escalators and I need help. Maybe you can catch people a few feet in front of me and get them to slow down some. People can only go down the escalators about two at a time." The guard gave me a nervous smile and started helping with the process.

Directing the crowd in this situation was one of the *most* difficult things that I have ever done. It was not that directing traffic up and down a couple of escalators in and of itself was especially difficult, but because of the incredible terror that we were all experiencing. People's emotions ranged from being totally dazed, to screaming and crying. I tried to put on a calm face, and even gave high fives to some of the people as they approached the escalators. "You're almost out of here," I said. "Keep moving, get out and go home. When you get to the bottom of the escalators make a left."

I was also screaming over and over, "Focus on the escalator steps! I don't want you to fall!" But admittedly, that was not at all my primary concern.

My *real* motivation was to get everyone to focus on the steps in an effort to distract them from their instincts to look out of the mezzanine windows! I especially made an attempt to speak briefly with my Port Authority co-workers as they left - some I knew, and some that I didn't know but recognized.

All of these efforts were made in an attempt to make the focus the *evacuation*, not the gruesome sight on the plaza.

As time went on I found it impossible to follow my own advice. I couldn't help but gaze out of the windows whenever there was a momentary break in the traffic. All that I could see was burning debris and human remains. It was all so surreal. But we were making progress in evacuating the tower, and hopefully we could get everyone out before things could get worse.

Then the south tower attack, which I *still* didn't know about, began to take its toll.

Gina

While the events on the mezzanine of the north tower plaza were taking place, Gina was on the telephone with my mother and brother watching the coverage on television. Their conversation continued to be interrupted by phone calls regarding my whereabouts. By now the situation was in front of the whole world, and they were in a position that was no different than just about everyone else's. They were simply fearful but hopeful.

Chapter 5

9:59 A.M. - The South Tower Collapses

Ken

Our efforts to evacuate the north tower were *never* really brought under total control. Not that anyone could have expected otherwise. I was standing in an area where I could see very clearly what the destruction of the tower had done to the plaza, and was having an impossible time grasping what was going on.

Then the situation got significantly worse.

Out of nowhere came a ground-shaking, thunderous roar. I felt as if I was standing in front of an on-coming freight train. The south tower was beginning to collapse. The structure, which stood a quarter of a mile tall, was situated just one hundred and forty feet from the north tower. It fell entirely in about fifteen to twenty seconds.

Imagine that! A one hundred and ten story building falling in less than half a minute! And it all happened so fast that nobody had time to react.

At most I was only a couple of hundred feet from the eye of the storm—the evil black cloud that the television cameras filmed rolling up West Street chasing people who were attempting to escape the collapse.

When the south tower fell, the concussion blew out the windows at the base of the north tower. I can remember hearing screaming for a split second before the entire world went entirely dark and silent. I was literally knocked off my feet and onto my back. My eyes were burning and I was swallowing what tasted like thick chalk. The mezzanine was completely engulfed by smoke, dirt, and debris blowing from the south tower into the base of the north tower. It was so dark and the air was so thick that I could not see my hand in front of my face.

I began to crawl on the carpet hoping that I could somehow reach the perimeter of the tower. *The only way I can describe how it felt is to imagine yourself crawling along the bottom of a deep swimming pool with your eyes closed,* all the while having no clue as to where you are or where you are going. Crawling along the bottom of a pool knowing that your next breath could be your last.

The goal was simple. Survival.

As I crawled around, thoughts of my wife and my family flashed through my head. I remember experiencing the chilling fear that I was going to die, and that it would happen at the World Trade Center - my favorite office complex, home away from home, and the place where I met my wife. But even so, I continued to crawl around never opening my eyes. And after what seemed like forever I was about to give up.

I stopped on the carpet and stayed on my hands and knees for a few seconds to gather my thoughts. Debris was still blowing around, and I could feel it hitting my hardhat and clothing. Otherwise, I couldn't see or hear anything. Mercifully, after a while I began to hear a faint voice in the distance, and concentrated on making out where it was coming from and what it was saying. It was a fireman. He had some sort of microphone, and was screaming, "If you can hear my voice continue to come this way."

As I slowly crawled the voice became a bit clearer, so I continued in the general direction that I was facing. During the entire time I never opened my eyes. *And I knew that if I wasn't crawling in the right direction it was over for me.*

I was fortunate enough to eventually reach the north perimeter of the concourse, and I crawled along the window line moving my arms right to left feeling for the columns. After a while, I reached an open emergency exit door and crawled out onto the plaza. A fireman screamed at me to lie down for a few seconds until I could get some air and catch my breath. The dust was still thick but was beginning to rise. My goal was to catch a pocket of breathable air at the ground level while rubbing my eyes with my undershirt. I was able to remove just enough of the dirt from my eyes, to be able to faintly see around me.

Then I got up and ran. Unfortunately I ran in the wrong direction and headed toward the vicinity of the center of the plaza. Then my instincts began to tell me that I was running the wrong way. What I needed to do was find a stairwell down to the street somehow, and the fountain was the wrong direction to be headed. After I got close to it, I turned to run back toward the tower.

That's when I came face to face with a sight that will last with me forever.

There were dead bodies and body parts scattered around the plaza. Human beings had been dismembered and reduced to body parts. One particular gruesome sight appeared to be a torso from the waist up with the eyes wide open. My guess is that this person had been hit by sharp flying debris or blown apart in the airplane explosion. And to this very day I do not know if the others had jumped from the tower or were hit from falling debris when the north tower was struck.

Regardless, the entire scenario took on the feeling of a nightmare. It felt like something that I would wake up from and share with my wife. I actually convinced myself that I would wake up in the morning and tell Gina that I had a wild and gruesome nightmare, and then get out of bed and go to work. Surely, *none* of this could have been real.

I got back down on the ground to gather myself and noticed the United States Custom House located just north of the north tower. After about a minute or so I got up and ran as fast as I could until I reached the building. An overhang protected the external wall of the building, so for an instant it felt like a safe place to be.

At this point, I said mental goodbyes to my wife, my family and friends. Many of their faces ran across my mind as I scrolled through the names of the people who were closest to me. My only other thought was that this was going to be an awful way to die and that my time was up, and I was going to be another body on the plaza.

The feeling that my life was going to end right there is one that I will never forget. I would never wish the feeling of imminent death on anyone.

As I began to think about where to run I looked up and a couple of bodies fell out of the sky, hit the ground with a loud thud and laid there lifeless. Human beings falling out of the sky for hundreds of feet and hitting the hard ground! By now the fire at the top of the north tower had to be intense and people who had given up hope of escaping had to make an unthinkable decision to either burn in the fire or jump. They had probably held on for as long as they could before jumping.

Again, given my mental state, all of this was a part of the same incredible nightmare. I knew for certain I would soon wake up from it all.

My only hope was to make one more attempt to run. Fortunately, there was a stairwell that led down to the base of the tower on West Street. I pressed my hard hat down on my head as tightly as I could, and rubbed my eyes, which were still burning, and ran for the stairs. I remember grabbing the railing and sliding down the steps, doing more sliding and tripping than walking.

The street level was just a sea of emergency personnel. There were ambulances, fire trucks, police cars and emergency medical services units all around me. People were shouting and running in every direction, and the sound of police and emergency vehicle sirens was at a level that I had never heard before.

For a brief second, the scene around me was reminiscent of being in the middle of a snowstorm on a dark night. It looked like we were in the middle of a major blizzard. The ash and debris that had fallen from the towers made the street and vehicles look like they had been freshly covered by a heavy gray snowfall.

After attempting to sit on the sidewalk along the wall at the base of the complex to catch my breath, I was directed by a police officer to run westward toward the Hudson River and then north. I couldn't clearly understand what he was saying at first. After he repeated himself I started to tell him, "I've been up on the plaza and I'm out of breath. I need to sit for a while." He responded in no uncertain terms, "Get up and run toward the river! Move now! Move!! Move!!"

I got up and ran across West Street toward Battery Park City and the Hudson River. By then there were hoards of people walking and running north along the jogging paths. I attempted to run past them, and I wasn't really focusing on what was in front of me.

After about a block, I ran into a park bench and went flying over it landing on my side. All the while, I never lost my hard hat. A gentleman helped me up, and the first thing that I did was ask him if I could borrow his cell phone to make a telephone call to whom and for what purpose I had no idea. It just seemed logical that I should have been calling someone that I knew. Anyone.

He told me, "My cell phone has no signal. I tried to reach my wife and the signal is dead. Sorry, I can't help you." I figured that maybe he did not want to lend me his phone. However, he was nice enough to help me up from the ground and I appreciated his assistance. I simply said, "Thanks for helping me up" and continued on.

Along the jogging path people were crying and clearly dirty and disheveled. We all headed north past Stuyvesant High School and then back onto West Street. The high school had released the students and they looked as dazed as the rest of us. I could not figure out why an airplane accident at the World Trade Center would have necessitated sending the kids home from school. Maybe it was a simple safety precaution.

As we got just north of the high school, the entire experience got even stranger. A tall gentleman in a dark suit holding a microphone stopped me. He had a cameraman with him and started asking me a bunch of questions. Of all of the people headed up West Street why he was stopping me was hard to understand.

"Excuse me, were you just in the towers?" he asked. I responded, "Yes, I got out a few minutes ago." I answered whatever questions he had without giving much thought to what was going on, and then I dashed off in another direction. Maybe this guy was working on some project and was recording the event. In any case, he asked, I answered, and it was time to move on.

Gina

By now the conversation among Gina, Kris, and my mother was one of mere speculation. However, there was considerably more concern because the unthinkable had

43

happened. One of the towers had fallen. A building with thousands of people working in it had fallen, and people were killed and dying. They were speechless, and their only hope was that by then I had evacuated the north tower and was far from the scene.

Kris didn't actually see the south tower fall. He was in his office at the time, and when he heard that the tower fell he ran out to watch the television coverage. Then he returned to his office and got back on the phone briefly with Gina and my mother. After a few minutes he exited the conversation, and he tried to reach my brother-in-law Kenneth on his cell phone without success. Finally, all three of them were back on the telephone again.

So now there was reason to be concerned about two members of the family.

My family had so many unanswered questions. *Did I get the voice mail messages that they left for me? If so, did I leave the area in time to avoid the catastrophe? Did my brother-in-law evacuate the Department Of Immigration offices and get to Brooklyn safely, or would he have been in the subway on the Manhattan side of the river? If we did get out of the area, where did we go? Would we be able to make contact with our family to let them know we were actually safe?*

There were too many critical questions with no answers.

Chapter 6

10:28 A.M. - The North Tower Collapses

Ken

I cannot tell you precisely where I was when the north tower fell. I was probably down on West Street. However, given the timing of the events I know that I did not escape the collapse with much time to spare. And while it was all happening, I had *no* idea that anything had collapsed. In my mind the towers were still there, and my only concern was where to go next.

Incredibly, just after speaking with the man in the dark suit, I spotted Ernesto Butcher standing in the middle of West Street with a few Port Authority Police Officers. They were staring in amazement at the World Trade Center site several blocks south and talking about what to do next. I stood in place for a few minutes and spat out as much debris as I could, trying to get my breath back. Then I ran over to him and we hugged. Given that I had last seen him on the mezzanine of the north tower when we spoke by the escalators, it was a huge surprise to see him.

45

My first words were, "Some guy in a suit stopped me in the street and asked me where I worked and what I saw. I might have done something that could get me into trouble. I told the guy that I am a Port Authority employee, and I didn't get clearance from Media Relations to speak to him." The policy of the agency was that statements made to the media were to first be cleared by Media Relations. Looking back, it's almost laughable. At a time like that my greatest fear was getting into trouble at work. He looked at me, paused, and calmly said, "Don't worry about it."

After attempting to gain our bearings, we got into a Port Authority police car, and the officer sped through the Holland Tunnel headed to the Port Authority's Holland Tunnel Administration Building in lower Jersey City, New Jersey. We needed to get to a Port Authority location in order to have communications capability with our other facilities and any other points of contact.

I remember thinking that the police officer was crazy because he was speeding down the center line of the tunnel. Surely there had to be traffic in front of us. But there wasn't a single vehicle anywhere. Maybe it was because we were in the tunnel after the rush hour, and we were headed away from the city in the late morning.

Or maybe the officer was driving that way to impress the boss.

Gina

Gina and my mother saw the north tower fall on the news. As soon as it fell, Gina lost control and began to cry and scream. She believed that I would have stayed in the tower to help with the evacuation process, as opposed to leaving the scene as quickly as possible. My mother tried to calm her down, telling her that I would be fine. She told Gina that she would need to be strong for me when I finally contacted her. Gina tried to believe her, but doing so was not coming easily. I had been in the north tower and had not made contact with her.

Kris was still reasonably calm but reserved.

My mother attempted to convince Gina to go to a neighbor's house. Unfortunately, we did not know any of our neighbors, so she had no choice but to stay in the house alone. Then Gina got off of the telephone because she wanted to keep the line open in the event that I was attempting to contact her.

At that point all that they had was hope and faith. *On that day, at 8:46 a.m., the world went from me getting up and going to work like any other day to me possibly being killed in a terrorist attack.* The minutes began to feel like hours.

Gina got back on the telephone with Kris and my mother a few moments later. By now Kris had been able to reach my Aunt Kathy in the Boston area, and conference her in on the telephone call. While they were talking, he got off the line and contacted my cousin Genise, who lived in Fairfield on the other side of town from us. He explained the situation to her and asked her to leave her house as quickly as possible to be with Gina. She really needed to have someone with her.

Then the situation began to appear significantly worse sometime after 12:30 that afternoon.

Gina received a frightening telephone call from a member of the Port Authority staff who was among those attempting to account for the employees who worked at the World Trade Center. She was asked if she was married to me, and if I had made contact with her. Gina's initial response was that she had not heard from me, and then she asked, "You mean you don't know where he is?" The staff member told her that I was the only member of the aviation department's senior staff who had not been accounted for - the only one.

Needless to say, her worst fears began to take on the feeling of reality. I was unaccounted for and given her sense that I would have stayed in the building I indeed may have been killed.

The crying began all over again.

Chapter 7

Holland Tunnel Administration Building in Jersey City, New Jersey

Ken

When we arrived at the Holland Tunnel Administration Building, we immediately went inside to the operations desk, and were greeted by Holland Tunnel staff and an emergency medical services (EMS) team. "How are you feeling" they asked. I responded, "I'm absolutely fine." Then I went to find a telephone. After a while, I needed some air so I stepped outside of the building. At that point the EMS guys cornered me. "You don't look good and you need to be checked out," they said.

Admittedly I had no idea how I appeared to them, and I was still confused about the entire event. I told them that I needed to work. "I am a management person in our aviation department, and I need access to a phone in order to make some calls and to try to get information about what happened at the World Trade Center." I found myself digging through the dirt in my left pants pocket for my wallet figuring that if I showed them my I.D. card and proved that I was a management person they would surely leave me alone.

49

But the next part of the dialogue had to convince them that I was *really* on another planet.

I attempted to explain to them that a serious accident had occurred in New York. I said something to the effect of, "I don't know if you guys are aware of this but something happened in New York this morning. Apparently a plane of some sort hit the World Trade Center. Everyone had to be evacuated." I really believed that they were hearing all of this for the first time! They looked at me like I was absolutely crazy. "You need to let us take you to the hospital" they shot back. I argued again that something happened in New York and that I needed to make some phone calls.

Fortunately the EMS workers convinced me to at least sit down on the side of the stretcher, which was on the pavement by the rear of the ambulance. One minute I was sitting, and the next thing I knew I was laying on the stretcher looking up at the sky and being lifted into the ambulance. I don't remember if I decided on my own to go to the hospital with them, or if they made the *appropriate* decision to take me whether I wanted to go or not. Why they thought it important that I go was way beyond me. I felt they were clearly overreacting to how I appeared to them. In any case, we were on our way to the hospital.

St. Francis Hospital

Ken

When we arrived at the local hospital, the ambulance backed into the parking lot. When the rear doors opened and I was lowered to the ground something immediately struck me as being very odd. There were no vehicles in the parking lot. Along the outside wall of the hospital was a line of cots and hospital beds with medical personnel standing around. It was a *very* eerie sight.

My first thought was that the hospital had been evacuated, which made me wonder why they would have taken me there in the first place. Surely the ambulance had a radio and could communicate with the emergency room. Or maybe the staff was on a break, or there was a huge accident somewhere in Jersey City like a school bus crash or something. If that was the case *why was I going to the hospital?* I would do nothing more than take up valuable time and resources when clearly there were going to be more important things for them to deal with. Besides, I came over to New Jersey to go to work!

I started to feel that I should have stayed in New York.

The paramedics rolled me into the emergency room, and I was immediately treated by a nurse who sat me up and asked me a series of questions: "Where were you in the World Trade Center? How is your breathing? How do your eyes feel? Do you have any pain or discomfort?"

Much like I did when I first encountered the EMS workers, I informed him that, "There was some sort of accident in New York this morning. It happened in the north tower where I was working. I came to New Jersey with my boss, and I tried to get some work done but the 'ambulance guys' made me come to the hospital."

The nurse had me lay down on a bed. He flushed my eyes, and then he put me on some sort of oxygen machine designed to clear my lungs. I felt myself spitting up the debris I ingested, and after what seemed like hours (I have no idea how long I was on the machine) a doctor came in to check me out. He left the area and then the nurse flushed my eyes again. I continued on the machine for a while longer while my eyes were flushed every several minutes.

A while later the doctor came in to check me out again. *"Mr. Greene," he said, "Given what you ingested, and where you were when the towers fell, you probably had about five minutes or so before you would have blacked*

51

out." If I had blacked out, I would have been inside of the north tower on the mezzanine carpet when it fell.

My reaction was to tell him that he was mistaken. "I was just in the towers and I understand that an airplane accident happened," I responded, "I *know* that nothing has fallen. I was over there. I would know." He told me again that both of the towers were gone. This time my response was more irritated than informational. "You're wrong. You probably heard a ridiculous rumor that's being spread in the hospital." He tried to assure me one last time that the towers were gone, and that it would take a while before my head would be entirely clear.

I ignored him.

At this point I was convinced that everyone that I had come in contact with since running from the towers had lost their minds. No one was acting or speaking rationally. Some guy in a suit stopped me in the street amidst the chaos to ask me a bunch of questions that I don't even remember. Then the police officer raced through the tunnel to New Jersey for no apparent reason. When we arrived in New Jersey I was captured by some EMS workers who insisted that I go to the hospital, even though I was perfectly fine. And now after treating me, some misinformed doctor was now trying to convince me that the towers had fallen!

I knew that something dramatic had happened, but I just couldn't understand why everyone was reacting so strangely.

Fortunately, *I* was under control.

After being cleared by the nurse to leave the hospital I got up from the bed and went to the bathroom. For the first time I saw that I was completely covered in dust and dirt. My hair was virtually white, with a ring around my head from the imprint of the hard hat, and my face and clothes were also covered in dust and dirt. I remembered what had happened when the mezzanine of the north tower went dark, and I concluded that the dirt and debris that I was breathing at the time covered me as well. After washing my face and my hands and signing my release papers, I headed for the emergency room exit.

A hospital staff person asked me if I could be given a ride anywhere, and I said that I needed a ride to the local train station so that I could take the train over to New York. She told me that all of the transportation into Manhattan had been shut down since that morning.

Still nothing registered with me.

The next best option was for me to go to one of the Port Authority facilities in Jersey City. The Technical Center, located just a few blocks from the hospital and the Holland Tunnel, was the place that I wanted to go. The hospital staff arranged for their employee shuttle van to take me to the Technical Center after dropping their employees off at the local train station.

I got into the van with seven or eight other people and immediately noticed that everyone was exceptionally friendly. A woman got on and sat next to me. "You must be hungry. I have a sandwich in my bag that you can have. Please take it," she offered. Similarly, the woman across the aisle offered me a can of soda. I remember thinking that I had ridden trains and buses all of my life and had never met people this friendly - certainly not on the train from Connecticut. I thought that perhaps it was the way that hospital people acted because they care for patients.

In any case I said, "No, thank you" and went back to the same story that got me strange looks. "Did you hear about a plane accident this morning? There was an accident that happened in New York this morning," I said. "One of your doctors heard some crazy rumor that the towers had fallen, but I was in the city this morning and actually left the World Trade Center before I came over here." The woman sitting next to me just looked at me and didn't appear to know what to say. She was silent until we arrived at the

53

train station, and then she exited the van with everyone else and left me alone with the driver.

When we arrived at the Technical Center I was told by the security guard that all of the agency's senior staff was at the Port Authority Police Command Center, also located in Jersey City just a few miles away. I got a ride from the Technical Center to the Command Center with someone who to this day I do not remember.

Gina

It was now in the afternoon, and Gina was waiting nervously by the phone hoping for a call from me. My cousin Genise and her daughter had joined her and were keeping her company. Her objective was to stay positive and calm, which was becoming more and more difficult with every passing moment.

Chapter 8

The Command Center

Ken and Gina

When I arrived at the Command Center it began to sink in that something *significant* had indeed happened. I showed my employee identification at the security desk, and walked down the corridor to a big conference room down the hall.

When I entered the conference room I was struck by the fact that there were several staff members who were clearly disheveled, some with hair and clothing that was as dirty as mine. At that point it really began to hit me that something was *very, very* wrong. Clearly all of us had been through an experience of major proportions.

Everyone was either on the telephone or in one of several mini-meetings around the room. By now it was sometime after 3:30 p.m., and I was told that I needed to make contact with the airports and work with them to assess where they stood from a security perspective. It was at that time that I learned that all of the airports across the country had been closed since shortly after the accident at the World Trade Center.

While sitting at a conference table I thought that maybe I should give Gina a call. I needed to let her know that I wouldn't be home that night. I figured that by now she was probably aware of what had happened in New York.

Gina was in the bathroom brushing her teeth and did not hear the telephone ring. Genise heard it ring, and waited to hear who was calling on the answering machine. Gina was screening calls in an effort to keep the line open in the event that I called. As I began to leave a message Genise screamed for Gina to pick up the telephone. I had almost left a full message on the machine when Gina answered.

She greeted me with a combination of crying and laughter. "Hi," I said, "Something happened at the World Trade Center this morning, but I'm fine. I have to work late tonight because all of the Port Authority facilities are closed. We're working on security stuff. It may be a day or two before I come home."

Gina said that she had been waiting for my call. She was talking a mile-a-minute and sounded out of breath. "I've been so scared that something happened to you. I watched what happened on television, and then someone from your office called and asked me if I had heard from you. I didn't know what to do or think. I love you. I've just been waiting by the phone for what seems like forever." I jumped in and said, "I can't stay on the telephone very long. We need to keep as many lines open in the Command Center as possible. I'll have to call you later." She told me that she loved me, and I responded that I loved her as well.

"I have to get off of the phone too," she said. "There are a lot of people that I need to tell that you are all right. A lot of people need to know that I heard from you. I need to call your mother, brothers and sisters, and some other people." I said fine and goodbye, and I hung up the telephone not knowing that she had received a few dozen telephone calls.

I wondered silently for a moment why all of these people would have called her about me, and left messages for her to return. *And why would my mother and siblings be interested in knowing that I was working in New Jersey, and wouldn't be home for some period of time?*

And as far as Gina was concerned, during the course of our marriage I had worked very late hours on occasion. There were also times when I did not come home at night for work related reasons. This was just another one of those occasions, admittedly more serious than usual.

Now *Gina* wasn't acting entirely rationally. What was wrong with everyone? I dismissed her strange behavior and began calling the airports.

Ken

And then the reality of what happened finally hit me in the most shocking and disorienting way that I could have imagined.

About an hour after I began to work, all of the activity in the room was stopped for a brief moment. We were all gathered together and told that after an extensive effort to account for our employees who worked at the World Trade Center there were over two hundred who remained unaccounted for.

I asked a colleague standing next to me what happened that would have caused staff to be missing. He said to me in a low, soft voice, "We don't know for sure how many people were still in the tower when it fell." I responded in disbelief, "The tower fell?" He looked at me and quietly said, "They're both gone Ken, they're gone – you really don't know?" He explained to me in great detail that both towers had been attacked and destroyed by terrorists who hijacked airplanes, and that thousands of people were killed and missing.

57

The reality of the situation was that I didn't know. Surely it wasn't because no one had attempted to tell me. All along I simply couldn't grasp the depths of what had really happened! All of the 'strange' behaviors and conversations that I encountered throughout the day slowly began to make sense to me. The towers had been destroyed and untold numbers of people had been killed. The whole world was in shock and living through a nightmare.

In a span of about one hundred minutes, the north and south towers had been both struck and leveled.

Then the emergency room doctor's comment about my having 'five minutes at the most' began playing in my head like a tape recording. All of a sudden I got an incredibly sick feeling. I found myself staring off into space for several minutes at a time, unable to pick up the telephone and call anyone. After a while my eyes welled up, and I got up and went to a back area of the floor and sat in a corner by myself for quite a few minutes.

I had come close to dying and had not fully realized that fact. And it was all starting to become clear to me. It was me! I was the one who had been clueless the entire time.

I began to wonder how many of the people who were working with me on the mezzanine to evacuate the north tower got out alive. How many had the good fortune to either be near an emergency exit door or hear the fireman's voice when the world went dark and silent? I remembered many of their faces very clearly, and I thought about the security guard who had been working with me at the escalator bank. Unfortunately, I would never know who among them survived and who among them died.

There was nothing that I did on my own that saved me - I was simply lucky. If I had been crawling in any other direction I would have died. If I had simply been farther away from the emergency exit I probably would have died. The feeling was quite overwhelming, and I actually found myself shaking.

After a while, I went back to the conference room and started to make some phone calls. There were televisions on around the room, and pictures of the attack on the World Trade Center were being shown non-stop. Up until that point I had not bothered to watch the televisions, but now I found myself mesmerized by what was being broadcasted. The news station was broadcasting the first airplane hitting the north tower, approximately twenty to twenty-five floors above where my office was located. It was also showing the second plane hitting the south tower. It showed people jumping out of windows, and the crowds of people headed north on West Street trying to out run the huge billowing cloud of smoke that was at their heels.

I could not take my eyes off the television sets. Even while I was on the telephone, I watched the footage over and over again for hours as I worked, each time hoping to pick up on something that I had missed before. It was still shocking, unfathomable and impossible to believe.

Later in the evening I was told by a few of my fellow employees that footage of my 'interview' was being shown on the CNN news channel. At first I had no idea what anyone was talking about, and simply dismissed the comments. I was certain that I did not do any interviews... until I saw myself on CNN around two o'clock in the morning.

The interview had been conducted by John Slattery, the gentleman in the dark suit with the cameraman who stopped me on West Street as I was running away from the towers. It turns out that he was from the local CBS television news affiliate. I honestly did not remember what I was asked and how I responded, but there I was with a hard hat on, covered in dust and dirt and trying to catch my breath and answer questions at the same time.

Now I understood why he chose me to interview – I was covered in dirt and I was wearing a hard hat.

He asked me if I was in the towers, and I responded that I was among those in the stairwell of the north tower who were evacuated. I described the process of descending the stairs while evacuating the building as orderly until the point where we reached the mezzanine level. When asked how I felt I responded, "I'm alive. I'm alive. I'm going to go home and hug my wife." Then I bent over and began to spit out as much of what I had ingested as I could.

It was a very strange twist to an incredibly sad, sad day.

That night I got a little bit of sleep on a cot in an office in the building before starting work again. We were all working around the clock, and sleeping was generally limited to a few hours while continuing to focus on the needs of our facilities, and the status of our fellow employees who were unaccounted for. We were all faced with challenges that no one could have ever imagined, and the difficult journey had just begun.

Chapter 9

An Agency At Its Best

The Port Authority is led by a Board of Commissioners under the joint direction of the Governors of New York and New Jersey, and operates in a politically charged climate. The agency is largely comprised of career professionals who enjoy working in the government sector.

There is a level of pride and satisfaction derived from working in an organization that has such a direct impact on day-to-day life in the region. Over its long history the Port Authority had built and managed airports, tunnels, bridges, and other transportation facilities in the New York metropolitan area. Without question it has been a large contributor to the growth and development of the region.

Working at the Port Authority requires that you deal with a certain level of bureaucracy, which at times can be frustrating and even discouraging. The decision-making processes can be slow and complicated. And when you add to the mix the day-to-day challenges of managing a very complicated transportation network, you have an agency that is under constant scrutiny from the political structure and the traveling public.

As I stated previously, it takes a certain kind of resilience to work in such an organization. I believe that along with that resilience, the depth of institutional knowledge possessed by the staff was an important factor

61

in the agency's ability to deal with the loss of the World Trade Center. We lost our home and much of our history.

And more importantly, we lost eighty-four employees and contract personnel. Thirty-seven of these employees were police officers – the largest loss of life ever suffered by a police department in a single day in the history of the United States.

Eighty-four lives had been ended by a single act of incredible brutality. For all of us this event was devastating beyond belief, but we did not lose our spirit. We all knew that somehow we had to recover and find a way to go on with our lives.

When the times got the toughest we were 'an agency at its best'.

After 9/11, going to work was very difficult, but in retrospect, the best thing for me. I returned to work immediately after the attack, and I wasn't forced to sit at home for days or even weeks waiting for a new place to report to, or to watch 9/11-related coverage for hours at a time. I honestly don't know how well I would have handled being at home for a few weeks. There was a level of comfort at work. Never before did I have the appreciation for seeing fellow employees than I did after 9/11.

I would report to the Command Center, and like everyone else my first concern was finding out if there was any news regarding our employees who were unaccounted for. With every passing day it seemed like we got nothing but more bad news. There was news about employees whose bodies were recovered or who were still missing. On the one hand I felt a sense of relief just knowing that there was some level of closure regarding the fate of some of our colleagues. On the other hand, each bit of tragic information was a cold reminder of the devastation that had occurred. Every one of these people had a family. There were spouses and children involved, all whose lives had been changed forever.

It was a hard lesson that we learned: we need to demonstrate an appreciation for those who are significant to us whenever we can. We cannot assume that we can always do so tomorrow. They can be taken from us in a heartbeat. All of us in the agency knew this to be true... eighty-four times over.

We all seemed to have good and bad days, but we found ways to support each other both professionally and emotionally. There were times when people had a hard time focusing or just needed someone to talk to. Counseling was available to staff both formally and informally, and if you wanted to speak to a professional crisis counselor one was always available. I believe that the support programs put in place by the agency helped to effectively address employees' personal needs.

Sometimes counseling took on the form of simply stopping by a supervisor's office and talking about how we were feeling, and what our fears and concerns were.

Although it would have been easy to fall apart, we all persevered. Besides the efforts to manage the business for several months, there were funerals and memorial services for our fallen colleagues, and we all had continued concerns for the families of the lost employees.

And as bad as our experience had been there was still an unknown out there that was hanging over our heads. Could this happen again? Was this just the beginning of terrorist acts in our area?

Given what we had to endure both individually and collectively, I have to say that participating in the post-9/11 recovery effort was an incredible experience for me. The perseverance demonstrated by the staff in working through such a tragedy, while keeping the transportation network in the region functioning, was truly phenomenal.

At times we had our share of internal differences and debates about how to move forward in the new world. But the bottom line was that the staff pulled together and made an incredible extra effort to work through the challenges of making the traveling public safer and more secure. The agency showed its strength through the crisis and as an insider, I was proud to be a member of the organization.

I also witnessed firsthand the incredible efforts made by police, fire, and emergency services personnel to rescue people from the towers on 9/11, and recover bodies during the following several weeks. I have tremendous respect and admiration for their work and the sacrifices they made. During the worst terrorist attack in this country's history, these men and women showed what they are truly made of.

In particular, I will *never* forget the faces of those firefighters who I encountered heading up the stairwell when I was leaving the tower. I am sure that they died that day. They were true heroes.

By most estimates, approximately twenty five thousand people were saved on 9/11 largely due to the collective efforts of fire, police and emergency medical services personnel, as well as civilians who participated in the evacuation process. And although there has been a lot of praise for those who risked their lives in that tragedy, there have been people who have criticized the performance of the New York fire and police departments in particular because of the things that did not go right.

Clearly, there is room for improvement as plans are made and processes are put into place to deal with major catastrophes in the future. Quite appropriately, the Congress established a '9/11 Commission' to investigate the events of that day, and develop recommendations for improvements that can be implemented nationwide.

I fully support the efforts of the commission, and I can't imagine that anyone could find fault with their mission.

Clearly there were problems with fire and police radio and telephone communications systems that did not function properly. There were problems with communications within the towers during the evacuation process. And there were also problems with the city's 911 emergency call system regarding the response time to calls, and the availability of information about what was taking place. Every public official involved in the crisis recognizes there were *technology* and *systems* breakdowns.

However, I have a *major* problem with the 'arm-chair quarterbacks' who were not there, and who have sat back and criticized the *individuals* who were directly involved. Those critics have *absolutely no clue* about what was going on that day.

For example, 9/11 Commission member John Lehman stated during a hearing with former New York City Fire Commissioner Thomas Von Essen, and former New York City Police Commissioner Bernard Kerik, that the city's response to the attack was in his own words, "Not worthy of the Boy Scouts". It was a despicable comment in light of the efforts made by the emergency response agencies on that day, and demonstrated no regard for the many lives that were lost in the process.

Simply put, *you had to be there.* Television couldn't fully capture the event. Newspaper and magazine articles couldn't fully capture the event. Books couldn't fully capture the event, nor could pictures and interviews.

So to all of the critics *'you had to be there'.*

The Immediate Aftermath

As a nation, we went through an initial period of total shock, incredible sadness, and an awakening to how quickly the world can change. We experienced how human beings can be slaughtered in a quick strike terrorist event.

We were and continue to be very angry about the loss of almost three thousand lives, as well as the new constraints on our ability to move freely in this society. Airport security procedures have taken on the profile of those in place in countries that have traditionally fallen victim to terrorist attacks. Our civil liberties have been compromised, and there is more intrusion into our lives. The government can and will delve into people's personal histories and detain them—without specific evidence—simply because they may be suspected of having ties to terrorist groups.

In a lot of ways we saw the best of America immediately after 9/11. Most notable was how many of the conflicts between people seemed to be unimportant, and how the level of unity and civility among us improved.

We weren't white or black, Asian or Latino, Jewish or Catholic – we were Americans.

We weren't rich or poor, gay or straight – we were Americans.

We weren't Democrats or Republicans – we were Americans.

For the most part, we were respectful of one another, concerned for each other, and unified in our freedoms. We supported each other through our incredible feelings of loss, while we struggled to come to grips with the reality that our personal and national security was vulnerable.

We had a greater awareness of the importance of our families, and were more sensitive to prioritizing quality time with our loved ones and making the effort to be involved in their lives to the greatest extent possible. We made a point of telling them how much we love them, and that they are important to us. And we made the time to call friends and family, especially those we don't see or hear from regularly, just to say, "Hello, I'm thinking about you."

Americans were unified in the position that terrorism is *under no circumstances* acceptable. Our conviction was to capture Osama Bin Laden and destroy the al Qaeda network both domestically and overseas.

To a great degree, I shared each and every one of these sentiments. And I thought that maybe, *just maybe*, the shock of all that happened would motivate Americans to begin to honestly and constructively deal with many of the *internal* issues that have historically plagued this country. Maybe we would *finally* begin to put into practice the very mantras that we profess to believe in, and move beyond the conflicts that are a regular part of American life.

Instead, to a great extent it appears to me that many Americans have gone through the grieving process only to recede back to their pre-9/11 behaviors and attitudes. For them the 9/11 experience was an occurrence that heightened their feelings of patriotism, however they define it. God only knows how many people took to hanging the American flag from their car windows or across the picture windows in their homes to show their patriotism.

As I observed the manifestations of people's patriotism I often wondered how many of my flag waving fellow Americans would have me live next door to them without having an issue or a concern, or sit next to me on the train in the future for that matter. Especially the folks who were steeped in their own self-righteous indignation - the ones who typically amaze me the most.

One night as I walked home from the train station I wondered if the head administrator of the assisted living center in Fairfield who had 'no room at the inn' hung *his* flag out of his car window. My guess is that he did - many Americans have mastered the art of 'symbolism without substance'. Sometimes we do things to make us feel good *in spite* of the reality of our own behaviors. I guess that too many of us will forever find comfort in our ignorance.

The First Visit to Ground Zero

Shortly after 9/11, I had the opportunity to visit the World Trade Center site. In order to do so I had to go through several levels of security clearance about one half of a mile north of the site on West Street, and put on a protective breathing mask and goggles and a hard hat before walking south to the site.

As I got closer to the area, the street was full of construction workers who had put in very long days and nights working to clear the site, and dump trucks that were being used to cart away the debris. This particular day was very windy, and the dirt swirled in the air and kicked up from the street.

I stopped at a spot that had been the vehicular roadway entrance to the north tower from West Street. From that position I could see and feel the magnitude of what had happened. What was formerly a living and vibrant entity was reduced to a pile of twisted metal, with thousands of casualties buried in the wreckage and fires burning below street level. Looking up at the destruction was numbing.

I will especially never forget the distinct smell of death and human decay that emanated from the site as I stood on West Street. It was strong and pungent, even through the protective breathing equipment that I was wearing over my face. Quite honestly, the smell of death was more striking than the sight of the devastation.

On the day of my visit to Ground Zero, I came closer to falling apart than at any other time since 9/11. Sadly, I was staring at what was and will always be a mass gravesite for the approximately 2,800 people who died during the attack.

The Holidays

Almost two months later, it was slowly beginning to feel like we could get back to some level of normalcy in our lives. However, when November arrived I absolutely dreaded facing the holiday season. Thanksgiving, Christmas and New Year's Day approached rapidly and the five-week period could not go by fast enough. It was impossible to enjoy the holidays knowing that thousands of people were dealing with the deaths of their loved ones, and in so many cases had no idea if their remains would ever be recovered. And on a personal level, the recovery status of several of my own co-workers was still unknown.

Given what had occurred, celebrating the holidays seemed highly inappropriate.

However, in the interest of not wanting to ruin the holidays for my family I found myself pretending to share in their holiday spirit, while feeling guilty the entire time. Every morning I would convince myself to do whatever was necessary to get through the season without affecting everyone around me. I cannot remember another point in my life when I had to remind myself to focus on being sociable and conversational, and not let on that I really would have preferred not celebrating anything. As much as I love my family, the reality was that they were in a holiday mode and I was simply along for the ride. Hopefully I didn't ruin their celebrations.

Most people don't look forward to their *holidays* ending so that they can go back to *work*. I did, and several of my co-workers did as well. In many ways we became a close-knit family unto ourselves because of the shared experience, and the workplace became a home of sorts. For me, *reality* was what was going on within the four walls of the agency, and when I was on my own time I was outside of that reality. For several months the workplace was 'home', and my family residence was simply the place where I took a break before getting back to what really mattered. It wasn't until after the holidays that the relationship between work and home life began to fall back into some kind of reasonable balance.

February 11, 2002

Monday, February 11th was a particularly difficult day. We received the news that the remains of five Port Authority Police Officers, and an injured woman who they were carrying, were found in the ruins of the north tower.

69

They had been in the lobby area on the concourse level of the tower helping people escape the attack when it collapsed. These folks were true heroes.

By that time we had been receiving information about the status of our colleagues for   five months. Still, this particular news hit me pretty hard. Back on that day, I had been situated directly above those officers on the mezzanine level of the tower. Their bodies had been recovered in a location that was proximate to mine. If I had not found my way out, there was the remote possibility that I could have been found in the general area where they were located as well.

I started to think about what it would have been like for Gina and my family if they had received notification during that weekend that my remains had been identified. By then it would have been five months after trying to come to grips with what happened, and after suffering through the holidays and most likely having given up the hope of my body or some other type of identification being found.

My mood at work that day was quiet and withdrawn. It was a very, very long day.

When I got home that night I told Gina about the recovery of the police officers, and that in my mind if there ever would have been a day where she got news of my being recovered or identified in the tower it could have been the previous Saturday. She looked at me, and gave me a nervous smile and changed the subject entirely. It was a clear and concise answer in and of itself.

We wound up watching television that entire evening without having a conversation about anything. Or, I should say, the television watched us, and the four hours of total silence said it all.

At 11 o'clock that night we quietly went to bed. Tomorrow would be a better day.

Two Years Later

I have to admit that since 9/11 my personality has changed to a great degree.

On the one hand I do not have a fraction of the sense of humor that I had in the past. Anyone who has known me for a significant part of my life would probably tell you that I was among the first to tell a joke or find humor in a particular situation. From junior high school through college I was largely the class clown. But since 9/11 things that I find humorous are not to the level they used to be.

I can only surmise that seeing people die firsthand in such a graphic fashion, and experiencing the collective effect of the attack on people so close to me has left a lasting impression.

On the other hand, in some ways I've changed for the better. Little things don't bother me nearly as much as they did in the past. Simple things like sitting in traffic, getting stuck in the wrong line at the supermarket, or losing hot water in the shower in the past would really annoy me. Now they hardly register. And I have a greater appreciation for individuals, like firefighters, and police and emergency personnel and the men and women in the armed forces, whose livelihoods require them to risk their lives while facing dangerous circumstances.

I don't experience dreams or nightmares regarding 9/11, although Gina believes that I am much more restless after I fall asleep, and often toss and turn.

However, the following three specific things still take me back to that day.

First, there are seven songs that I remember hearing on the radio on my way to work that morning. Hearing any one of them today puts me right back on the 6:08 a.m. train headed to Grand Central Terminal.

The sound of bagpipes is another cold reminder. Three hundred and forty-three firefighters and sixty police

71

officers died on that day, and the traditional funeral includes a processional accompanied by musicians in Scottish kilts playing bagpipes. The song that most often comes to mind for me is Amazing Grace. Whenever I hear bagpipes I quickly find a way to change the channel or turn the sound down. It's not that I don't like that music. It has taken on a different meaning to me since the events of 9/11.

And last but not least, are thunder and lightning storms. There was a time when I could sleep through virtually anything. Gina believed that I could sleep through a rock concert in my own living room, and she was probably correct. However, at this point I can't sleep whenever there is thunder and lightning. I don't even stay in bed. The noise and vibration gives me the same feeling that I had when the south tower collapsed. Fortunately, it doesn't happen often. The last time that we had such a storm, which was at 2:00 in the morning, I got out of bed and watched television until I needed to get ready for work.

I know that I have fared significantly better than others who have suffered lasting physical and psychological damage, and I feel for all of them.

The most significant change is that I am much less tolerant of the institutional racism and hypocrisy that continues to be perpetuated in too much of our society. My personal experience on 9/11 has made me much more likely to confront ignorance in a more direct and 'in your face' manner. I am much more likely to challenge folks about their attitudes and behaviors, especially those who haven't learned anything from the experience of 9/11.

Simply put:

If the events of September 11, 2001 haven't made folks wake up and examine the manner in which we all relate to each other, nothing will.

Chapter 10

I Know…. Let's Blame The Middle-Easterners!

Unfortunately, but predictably, the reaction in this country has largely been that because the terrorists were of Middle Eastern descent, all people from that part of the world are potential terrorists. Many Americans believe that this country has historically been 'gracious' enough to allow people from around the world to live here, and that this is how they thank us. They believe the terrorists came here under the pretext of seeking liberty and freedom, and instead tried to take us down. They attempted to intimidate us by destroying a national symbol of what we stand for and killing thousands of people in the process. We are very angry and equally confused. Many Americans find it impossible to believe that any group of individuals, or entire nations for that matter, could hate us so much that such an attack could be conceived and carried out.

73

A few weeks after 9/11, I had a conversation with a colleague of mine about the attack, and he shared his feelings with me regarding what the country should do in response. He was insistent that because of what happened *all* people living in America who were of Middle Eastern descent should either be incarcerated or sent back to the country that they or their ancestors came from.

"I have absolutely no guilt about my feelings," he told me, "and I know that *most* people in this country feel the same way. I don't have anything against those people. I just can't trust them anymore. You can't tell which ones are good and which ones are potential terrorists. If they hate us so much they should just leave, or maybe we should make them leave. We have to protect ourselves."

I hate to say it, but he was probably correct about his belief that many Americans felt the same way that he did.

He happened to live in a neighborhood in Queens that is home to a number of families of Middle Eastern descent, several of whom lived on the same street with him. "My kids go to school with children from these families, and I will no longer allow my children to play with *them* after school," he said. He was also going to cut off all contact with his next door neighbors, both of whom were doctors born in Pakistan.

After listening to his rant I calmly responded.

"Let me see if I understand you correctly," I began, "It's your position that if a terrorist is a member of a certain ethnic group then all people like them should be branded as potential terrorists and thrown out of the country. Or at the very least, you would make sure that you and your family have nothing to do with people of the same ethnicity in order to protect yourselves." He emphatically responded, "Yes, I hate to say it but that is how it would be. No questions asked."

I continued the conversation. "Do you have any brothers or sisters?" I asked. He stated that he had a sister in college and a younger brother in his mid-twenties who lived and worked in the south. I quizzically asked him, "How difficult was it for you to cut off all contact with your brother a few years ago? And how about anyone else his age, you know, other relatives, friends, neighbors, or people that you come into contact with from time to time?"

He was totally baffled, and simply stared at me with no clue as to what I was talking about. I added, "I can't imagine how hard it was for you to explain to your children why their uncle and people like him were no longer welcome in your home, that they were potential terrorists and would never be allowed to have contact with the family again. And harder still, how did your brother feel when you told him that he should be forced to leave the country?"

His confusion turned to mild anger and he firmly stated, "I have no idea what you're talking about. I don't have any issues with my brother. And what do you mean to infer that he could be a terrorist?"

Now I was 'confused'.

I told him that I was only following *his* logic, so it stood to reason that his brothers and every white male of about the same age were suspected potential terrorists.

Why?

"Do you remember a guy by the name of *Timothy McVeigh?*" I asked, "Do you remember him? The twenty-six year old white male *terrorist* who bombed the Alfred Murrah Federal Building in Oklahoma City in April 1995? You know, the guy who drove a car bomb to the building one morning and killed one hundred and sixty-eight people? Given that he was a *terrorist* it only follows by your reasoning that *all white males* around his age should also be considered potential *terrorists*, and at the very least should be sent back to the country of their ancestors."

Predictably, silence and a blank stare was all that I got. "You're not telling me that you still associate with your brother and other people in his age group are you? You're not that much of a hypocrite are you?" I asked with a smile. And by now he was candy apple red. "Help me understand. Your position on the matter is what?" I continued.

He did the very thing that the narrow minded ignorant and bigoted types typically do when their highly intellectual thinking is challenged: he walked away from me. I stayed put for a moment, and then I joined my beloved fellow countryman at the coffee station. He was mumbling to himself, probably feeling embarrassed by his inability to follow his own thought process to a logical conclusion, and his failure to respond to me without sounding like an idiot.

Then he offered up a response that I could have never dreamt up myself. With a straight face he said, "But McVeigh was an American, not some immigrant." And then he walked away. Incredible. In other words, an American terrorist was OK; it was those foreign terrorists that he had a problem with!

I eventually concluded our conversation with a little historical perspective.

I told him that it is a historical fact that unless his family was of Native American descent, or unless he was a descendent of the Africans who came over on slave ships, he and his family are *immigrants* a few generations removed, and no different than his neighbors and their children. Then I suggested that given that his neighbors are probably more tolerant than he was maybe *he* should pack his own bags for the 'homeland'.

Needless to say, from then on he always found a way to avoid me.

It has always amazed me how self-righteous so many Americans are. So much so that they can take positions on issues that are totally irrational, and actually feel good about themselves while doing so! For many of us, like my co-worker, our perspectives are not a matter of '*what*' we know to be right or wrong. They are simply a matter of the '*who*' that is involved.

Let's be for real: if *all* people of a certain racial or ethnic background were held accountable for the actions of a few there would be nobody left to live in this country! It's easy to take the hard line with those whom we believe are 'different' from us when something negative happens without taking a good look in our own backyard.

And time and time again I hear the same hypocritical argument. *Put them all in jail, or send them back where they came from.* Funny, the one thing that I have never heard is that *all people of European descent* should be sent back to Europe because of individuals like Timothy "The Oklahoma City Bomber" McVeigh, Theodore "The Unabomber" Kozinski, Ted "The Serial Killer" Bundy, John "The Serial Killer" Wayne Gacy, Jeffrey "The Cannibal" Dahmer, or Charles "The Ladies Man" Manson.

How many Americans have ever been leery about flying on airplanes with folks who look like *these* murdering terrorists? How many have cut off associating with folks who bear a resemblance to them?

When two students at Columbine High School in Littleton, Colorado, who were members of the 'trench coat mafia,' killed fourteen fellow students and one teacher, and wounded twenty-three others in a hail of gunfire in 1999, I don't seem to recall the sentiment being that all socially alienated white teenagers should be rounded up and incarcerated or deported to the land of their ancestors!

In fact, it became public knowledge *after* the shootings that the Jefferson County Sheriff's Office in Colorado had several warnings *prior* to the massacre that these teenaged '*terrorists*' were trouble.

The Colorado Attorney General stated that the county sheriff's office had *fifteen* dealings with these teenagers, including a 1998 arrest for breaking into a van, as well as vandalism and threats made against people in the community. In addition, approximately five months before the killings, the 'terrorists' made a videotape walking through the hallways of the high school in trench coats and sunglasses, attempting to portray hit men who could be hired by their classmates to murder bullies in the school. They had actually been recorded screaming vulgarities into the camera promising to brutally kill their intended victims.

Was there any outrage among the students or adults who were aware of this behavior or the school administration for that matter? Of course not. They were just a couple of 'kids from the comfy suburbs' (as opposed to the urban core), so why worry?

Try to picture a couple of minority students attempting to pull this stunt at Columbine High School, or any other high school for that matter. They would have been face down on the floor with a knee in their backs and handcuffs on, and on their way to a holding cell. Dreaded minority kids make people nervous on a normal day, so I can't imagine any other treatment in such a situation.

Clearly, it's the old double standard.

And as for the notion of 9/11 being the first act of massive terrorism on American soil in our history we quickly leap over a piece of the past. Under what category would we place the Ku Klux Klan? Are they not *terrorists*? Their 'contribution' to history was lynching blacks, Jews, and other so-called 'non-Americans' in the interest of preserving the sanctity of white power, and keeping the race pure and uncontaminated. All the while they professed to stand on the principles of Christianity, running around in their hoods and setting fire to homes and churches in an attempt to kill and intimidate out of pure hatred.

Maybe I'm missing something. To this very day there are still Klansmen in this country actively looking to grow their membership back to historical levels. According to the

Southern Poverty Law Center in Montgomery, Alabama, which monitors hate groups and extremist activities under a project named Klanwatch, there are still over seven hundred such hate groups still active around the country.

At what point will our government deploy the military to bomb and destroy *their* training camps? When will our honorable freedom fighters mobilize troops to capture *their* leaders and imprison them until they break down and provide information about their organizations?

And at what point in time will a president, any president, address the nation and tell us that 'America is the land of freedom. All men are created equal, with liberty and justice for all. The Ku Klux Klan and organizations like it have had decades to cease and desist, and have failed to do so. As your commander and chief I am ordering the armed forces to attack their bases of operations to destroy them'?

The answer is *never*. And the expectation is also never. We simply pay lip service to this brand of racism and terrorism *internal* to this country because, as my astute former colleague in the workplace stated, "they're Americans, not some immigrants".

When police officers shoot and kill or injure unarmed individuals, who are historically disproportionately minorities, because they 'supposedly' and incorrectly believe that they are in danger, where is the outcry? And why do these officers too often think that they are in danger? Do I need to state the obvious?

The police will typically be protected by their union, the mayor, and other politicians. A person caught stealing a cheap sweater can end up getting more jail time than a law enforcement officer who makes such a 'mistake' without provocation.

I am a college educated professional person who has never been charged with or even accused of committing any sort of crime. To this very day, even after the post 9/11

79

'united we stand' proclamations, my antenna still goes up whenever I see a police car in the vicinity. It's not that I have done something wrong or that I am contemplating a crime, it's because I have been stopped in the past for no good reason. I know that assumptions are made that I am a potential criminal because of the manner in which black males are typecast.

Besides, getting stopped, harassed, billy-clubbed, or being handcuffed and thrown into the backseat of a police car would probably interfere with my trip to Walmart!

When I go into certain stores, I am *still* followed around by sales people who offer up the transparent 'can I help you' line. In some cases they will ask me once, twice, three and even four times! Typically, they will stand behind me in the same aisle while everyone else in the store has plenty of space to circulate and look at the merchandise. There can be several other customers in the store and I am the one person with the constant company, or more realistically, under surveillance. Lucky me. I'm so special that I merit my own personal shopping valet.

I have even had sales people peak around the corner of the aisle at me like they are playing a spy game. In such cases I would turn around slowly knowing that they would pull their head back. The entire exchange takes on the ridiculous feeling of playing 'hide and go seek' with my three-year-old nephew.

Typically, after a while I pleasantly say something like, "Look, I don't plan to steal anything, and I promise not to buy the house next door to you, date your daughter, or go to your church. I simply want as much space as everyone else in the store to shop comfortably." Always with a smile.

Predictably, the defense mechanism surfaces. "Sir, um, I'm not worried about you taking anything – I just thought that you, um, might need help" they will typically respond.

Sure. Right.

Then I'll ask, "Is it that I look lost or stupid to you? You seem to feel that everyone else in this section of the store can differentiate between small, medium, and large sweaters on his or her own. And you haven't spent one minute with the other customers. Can you tell me why?"

Almost always I get the blank stare that I have become so accustomed to, and I continue, "Maybe I'm missing something. It must be the complexities involved in the art of sizing sweaters. I missed that class while I was in graduate school. Since I have your undivided attention, could you review with me the significance of small versus medium versus large? Will I need to take notes? I want to make sure to get it right. It might also be helpful to my wife. She gets followed around in this store too."

And then I'll ask, "Have you got a pad and a pencil that I can borrow?"

You could probably guess by now what happens next. They walk (run) away from me.

The shame of it all is that the likes of Rambo could have walked into that store at the same time, dressed in army camouflage, carrying an Uzi rifle in his arms with grenades strapped around his waist, and the salespeople would not have had him under surveillance!

He could have probably stuffed a bunch of shirts into his bag and shot a few lights out while screaming 'you're all dead men,' and still no one would have been concerned.

But I'm in the store, and surveillance is required!

Now I know the difference between being helped and being followed. All of us from time to time encounter aggressive sales people who are in our face. But some of us receive too much unjustified attention too much of the time.

This is supposed to be the land of fair and consistent treatment of all people. Am I missing something?

81

PART II. POLITICS

Chapter 11

Brother Gov, Can You Steal An Election For Me?

Among the biggest catastrophes in the post 9/11 world is none other than George W. Bush. And although much of the focus has been on his performance during his occupancy of the White House, we shouldn't forget how he got there in the first place.

His road to the White House is a clear demonstration of the lack of honesty and integrity that are at the core of the Bush family's legacy. In particular, the 2000 presidential election in Florida was the beginning of the race and power game that has been the basis for his time in office.

Four years ago, if you had asked me what the largest thing that a person could possibly steal could have been I probably would have said a tractor-trailer or a mobile home, or maybe a modular house sitting on one of those huge trucks that I have seen on the highway.

But a state election? And by extension a United States presidency? I would have never dreamt that such a feat could actually be pulled off.

That is, not until George Bush, Jr. from Texas stole the 2000 statewide presidential election in the State of Florida, the one state in this country that 'just happened' to have his brother Jeb Bush as its governor.

What a cozy coincidence. Bush's 'Brother Gov' just happens to be from Florida.

Florida is a state where voting patterns have historically been markedly different between black and white voters. Unlike the majority of Florida residents, black voters, who represent approximately twelve percent of the population, had *overwhelmingly* voted for democratic candidates in the past and were expected to vote heavily for Al Gore in the presidential election.

Given this expectation, there was a concern in the Republican Party that Bush could lose the Florida election to Gore. But fortunately for him, 'Brother Gov' was in control, so the chances of stealing the election were good if the process could be rigged to eliminate historically democratic voters. And who better to eliminate than black folks?

In preparation for the election, Florida Secretary of State Katherine Harris, who reported to 'Brother Gov', hired a company by the name of Database Technologies (DBT), which just happened to be a *'Texas'* based operation, to conduct a comprehensive analysis of the state's voting rosters. Coincidently, she was also a co-chairman of the Bush presidential campaign in Florida and a member of the State Board of Canvassers, which oversaw the statewide election process.

Harris directed DBT to verify that the Florida residents who were listed on the voting rosters as felons had in fact been convicted of felony offenses, and were correctly flagged as not being eligible to vote. The laws in Florida prohibited convicted felons from voting in the election.

DBT had extensive background checking capabilities with a network of approximately twelve hundred databases that could have been used to verify personal information regarding Florida residents. However, the company was instructed *not* to use its databases in order to conduct its review. Instead, DBT was directed by 'Kathy the Kleptomaniac' Harris to acquire names from Internet sources, including the names of convicted felons from several other states.

Subsequent to acquiring information from the Internet, DBT began its analysis by first focusing on Florida residents. The data was full of errors and included the names of people who had *not* committed felonies but were nevertheless about to be denied the opportunity to vote. It was so full of errors that it included names like Linda Howell from Madison County, the same individual who happened to be an *elections supervisor* in that county!

In all, it was estimated than at least fifteen percent of the fifty eight thousand names in the database (approximately seven thousand people) were incorrectly categorized as having felony charges on their records.

This information was also used to eliminate the voting eligibility of Florida residents whose names were '*similar*' to those of felons listed in the other states. In addition to reviewing personal characteristics such as date of birth and gender, these names were matched by *race*, which effectively made it easy to be selective regarding individuals who would be eliminated from the list of eligible voters. So if Luther Jackson from *Ohio* was a registered felon, then someone named Luther Jackson from *Florida* was going to be denied the right to vote.

And to add to the remarkable series of coincidences, the other states whose databases were utilized by DBT just happened to include, you guessed it, *Texas*.

Another eight thousand residents who had committed *misdemeanors* in other states before moving to Florida were also counted as *felons*. They were eliminated from the eligible voters list even though they legally had the right to vote with only misdemeanors on their records.

As a result of that process, it was estimated that approximately *sixty thousand* individuals were eliminated from the voting eligibility ranks by 'Kathy the Kleptomaniac' *before* the election even took place. And the majority of these voters were black.

Step one had been accomplished: legitimate black voters had been eliminated from the election pool, increasing the possibility of Bush winning the statewide election.

Election Day 2000

Several months later, November 7th arrived. It was Election Day, and things really got ugly.

Floridians went to the polls all across the state and thousands of them were in for a big surprise. Even though they were entirely within their rights to vote it wasn't about to happen on that day. When many of those honest, law abiding citizens reported to the sign-in desk in their local polling station they were informed that they would not be allowed to vote because they had felony offenses on their record. These claims were absolutely false, but at that point there was nothing that they could do about it.

In some precincts witnesses reported that they had been intimidated when they went to the polls by police officers who put up roadblocks near their polling stations. *Ironically, these roadblocks were set up around stations in predominately black communities.*

I guess the assumption was that black people were less capable of going to the polls in an orderly fashion than the rest of the population.

There were even problems in polling stations where people *actually* voted, especially in stations where paper ballots were read electronically. And the problems clearly had racial overtones. For example, the contrast between the way that Gadsden County and Leon County voters were treated at the polls, all of whom submitted paper ballots, was an absolute disgrace.

Approximately fifty-seven percent of the population in Gadsden County is black. In that county ballots submitted with any extra markings on them were deemed to be invalid no matter how slight the markings were, and were not counted in the vote tabulations.

Ultimately, one out of every eight votes submitted in that county was thrown out. One out of every eight!

Leon County, home of the state capital Tallahassee, also had difficulties with the use of the same paper ballots. Approximately sixty-seven percent of this county is white, which is almost the polar opposite of Gadsden County. Residents in this county were historically much more likely to vote for Republican candidates in a presidential election.

As was the case in Gadsden County, there were voters in Leon County who submitted ballots with extra markings on them. However, in their polling stations the ballots were being read *before* they were secured. If the voters incorrectly marked their ballots they were allowed to re-submit a new one.

As a result, only one in *one hundred* votes were thrown out. One in one hundred!

Let's see. In largely black Gadsden County the votes were secured immediately, voters were not informed if their ballots had been thrown out, and no one was allowed to recast their vote. But in largely white Leon County they were allowed to recast their vote.

In Palm Beach County nineteen thousands votes were discounted, and in Duval County twenty-seven thousand votes were discounted. Of this number over twelve thousand of the discounted votes came from polling districts where the population was over ninety percent black, and many of the votes that were discounted happened under questionable circumstances.

There is no way that all of this could simply have been confusion. At every turn in the process the so-called confusion happened to disaffect black voters the most, and their ability to vote was denied in one fashion or another.

But that's not all. There was even more shady stuff going on with the election.

By Florida law, absentee ballots are eligible to be included in an election if they are either postmarked or signed on or before Election Day. Historically, most absentee ballots are cast by overseas military personnel who typically vote for republican candidates. It is estimated that about twenty-five hundred of these votes were included in the vote count, even though as many as seven to eight hundred *did not* meet the legal requirements for inclusion.

There were also claims that in Seminole and Martin Counties members of the Republican Party were allowed to fill in missing information on absentee ballots to insure their inclusion in the total vote count!

But I guess that 'Brother Gov' and 'Kathy the Kleptomaniac' had broken so many laws and trampled on so many people's rights that they were too far gone to even worry about potential consequences. Besides, they were so close to pulling off the scam of the century that apparently nothing else mattered.

So the election went just as the Bush plan was designed to have happen. They threw out *legal* votes that were most likely to go to *Gore*, and included *illegal* votes that were most likely to go to *Bush*!

And The 'Winner' Is?

In the early evening on Election Day the major television stations began declaring that Al Gore had won the Florida election. But by 2 o'clock in the morning the projections changed and it appeared that George Bush was the winner. Based on the new projections, Gore called Bush and conceded the election, only to learn shortly thereafter that Bush's lead had narrowed to a number that was less than one half of one percent. Under Florida law an automatic recount is required under such circumstances.

At 4 o'clock in the morning, the news networks withdrew their projections about who won the election. The entire election process had been reduced to mass confusion, and a number of serious concerns about the manner in which the election was conducted quickly surfaced.

Among the most significant problems was the ballot that was used in Palm Beach County. Those ballots were so poorly designed that errors in the voting process were inevitable. There were ten names on the ballot, which was designed with two facing pages and punch holes down the center. The holes didn't always line up with the arrows that pointed to the candidate's names, so it was easy to be confused about which name was being selected.

Consequently, a large number of errors were made.

A subsequent audit of these ballots was conducted for cases where voters incorrectly punched holes for more than one candidate. It turned out that roughly 8,200 individual votes were cast for both Gore and another candidate, and roughly 1,600 individual votes were cast for both Bush and another candidate. As a result, the net loss for Gore was approximately 6,600 votes, almost ten times the number of additional votes he would have needed to win the election.

It also came to light that voting machines in a number of counties across the state failed to count legitimate ballots.

So the game was not entirely over, and the saga was going to go on for at least another month. The recount process was to begin with votes cast in several counties selected by Gore as mandated by Florida state law.

Clearly the Bush team was afraid of what would happen if an *accurate* recount was conducted. So what did Mr. Bush do? He had his lawyers run to the courts and attempt to stop the recount process!

Time to Appeal to the Legal System

On November 13th, the Bush team presented its case to a federal judge that a recount could not be conducted fairly and accurately, and the judge ruled against them. However, there was a disagreement between the Florida Attorney General's Office and 'Kathy the Kleptomaniac's' Office over the justification for recounting votes, so a decision was ultimately made to stop the process until the courts could resolve the conflict.

And then 'Kathy the Kleptomaniac' tried to pull another fast one in order to control the official outcome.

She let the world know that recounted votes submitted after the November 14th election certification deadline would not be counted toward the election results. This was another blatant attempt to subvert justice!

To add insult to injury, on November 18th she actually attempted to certify Bush as the winner. However, the Florida Supreme Court stopped her plan, because it had not yet ruled on Gore's appeal for a recount. And on November 21st the court decided to extend the certification deadline by twelve days, which gave Gore five days to identify enough votes to rightfully claim the election.

Given this development Bush appealed again, this time to the United States Supreme Court!

On November 24th, the Supreme Court agreed to hear the Bush team's appeal to invalidate a recount, and on December 3rd Bush moved the appeal process forward. Subsequently, the Supreme Court disallowed the extension of the certification deadline and directed the Florida Supreme Court to clarify the basis for its decision to allow a recount. In other words, they had to cite a good reason why a recount was necessary.

The U.S. Supreme Court needed a clarification. Let's see. How about the fact that several thousand Floridians were denied their legitimate right to have their votes counted in the election? How's that for a clarification?

On December 8th, the Florida Supreme Court ordered a hand count of approximately nine thousand ballots in Miami-Dade County that had not been double checked after the voting machines had registered them as non-votes. The court also ordered that the results of partial recounts that had already been taken in two counties be added to the votes that had been officially certified. These votes would have cut Bush's alleged lead over Gore to less than two hundred with several thousand votes left to be counted, most of which would likely have been cast for Gore.

The *total* recount would have included over forty-three thousand votes in as many as sixty counties, and was to have been completed by the afternoon of December 10th.

In the meantime, democratic and republican staff members from Washington D.C. based campaign offices prepared to fly to Florida to help oversee the recount process. Their goal was to ensure that it was handled correctly while meeting the December 10th deadline. If necessary, the recount process was going to be performed around the clock.

Bush was *clearly* on his way to losing his alleged lead because the interest of the court was to simply see that *all* of the residents of Florida were given a fair and equal opportunity to have their votes count in the election. Clearly, that is, until the U.S. Supreme Court acted again.

On December 9th the U.S. Supreme Court, by a vote of five to four, *stopped* the recount process that had been ordered by the Florida Supreme Court pending their review of the case. The court also ordered that attorneys for both Bush and Gore be prepared to present oral arguments before them on December 11th in order for the Supreme Court to make a final decision. This step was taken as if the oral arguments were really going to matter.

The court's final ruling should not have been the least bit surprising. The U.S. Supreme Court is comprised of nine judges. Seven of these judges were appointed by Republican presidents, while two were appointed by Democratic presidents. The five justices who voted to *stop* the recount process (along with the presidents who appointed them) were Anthony Kennedy (Gerald Ford, Republican), Antonin Scalia (Ronald Reagan, Republican), Clarence Thomas (George Bush Sr., Republican), Sandra Day O'Connor (Ronald Reagan, Republican), and chief justice William Rehnquist (Richard Nixon, Republican).

And on December 12th, by a vote of five to four, the U.S. Supreme Court officially handed George Bush the presidential election. Five of the seven Republican judges voted to install Bush. And how did they explain this decision to the American public?

Justice Scalia wrote the final opinion that said:

"The counting of votes that are questionable legally does, in my view, threaten irreparable harm to petitioner (Bush) and to the country, by casting a cloud upon what he claims to be the legality of his election. Count first, and rule upon legality afterwards, is not a recipe for producing election results that have the public acceptance democratic stability requires."

91

"Because it is evident that any recount seeking to make the December 12th date will be unconstitutional...we reverse the judgment of the Supreme Court of Florida ordering the recount to proceed...It is obvious that the recount cannot be conducted in compliance with the requirements of equal protection and due process without substantial additional work."

Let me translate the decision for you.

"The fact that an event of the magnitude and importance of a United States presidential election was about to be stolen by a candidate, and the fact that thousands of citizens had their constitutional rights violated in the process really doesn't matter. If we allow the votes to be recounted after our desired candidate has been anointed as the winner, and we find out that he was the loser, it will harm him regardless of the fact that he *legitimately* lost the election. And besides, a deadline for counting votes is required to be met, and there would have been too much work to meet it."

Justice Scalia's position was that the deadline had to be met because the election was governed by the Constitution, the same Constitution that allegedly guarantees equal protections under the law. However, these protections were denied to thousands of largely black citizens in Florida, who historically vote overwhelmingly for the democratic candidates in presidential elections.

These citizens were illegally scratched from the roster of eligible voters under the direction of Katherine Harris, the same Katherine Harris who was co-chair of the Bush presidential campaign in Florida, a member of the Board of Canvassers that oversaw the election process, and the Florida Secretary of State under Governor Jeb Bush. The same Jeb Bush who is the brother of George Bush Jr., who happened to be the same George Bush Jr. who was running for president.

What was Justice Scalia's assessment of that factor in the election process? And did the Supreme Court focus on the well-documented denial of the opportunity to vote to legitimate Floridians? No.

Did the Supreme Court focus on the well-documented illegal inclusion of overseas ballots cast after the deadline period? No.

Did the Supreme Court focus on the well-documented inclusion of defective ballots in some voting stations and not others? No.

Normally a court will focus on addressing its technical findings as well as its decisions. Not this time. It didn't give us the old, 'the facts aren't quite clear, um, uh there are two sides to every story, um, uh the preponderance of the evidence indicates things were done correctly.' I wonder why?

The Supreme Court defended its decision based on the so-called potential to hurt George Bush's *feelings* and the difficulty in meeting a *deadline.*

The bottom line to this scam was that Bush had *stolen* the Florida election by what was certified to be *five hundred and thirty seven* votes. As a result, he was going to be able to acquire enough *electoral* votes to steal the presidency by a margin of two hundred and seventy-one to two hundred and sixty-seven, which was a single electoral vote more than is required to win a presidential election.

Had Al Gore been treated justly he would have won the electoral vote count by a margin of two hundred and ninety-two to two hundred and forty-six. Gore also happened to win the popular election by about five hundred thousand votes.

But none of that mattered. Bush and 'Brother Gov' found a way to eliminate thousands of predominately black voters from the process.

As it turned out, in a state with a black voting population of approximately *eleven* percent a whopping *fifty-four* percent of the votes that were rejected were cast by black folks!

It also turned out that approximately ninety percent of the blacks who were allowed to vote voted for Al Gore. Assuming that the voting pattern would have remained the same (which is a reasonably safe assumption), among the several *thousands* of blacks who were illegally denied the ability to vote, only seven to eight *hundred* more black votes would have been required to beat Bush.

The Supreme Court's decision effectively ended any chance that Al Gore had of finding justice and rightfully claiming the position of President of the United States.

United States Civil Rights Commission

Allegations of election improprieties were also brought by black voters before the United States Civil Rights Commission, which agreed to conduct an investigation in January 2001. The charges were that illegal measures were used to deny thousands of blacks the ability to vote.

Several witnesses appeared before the committee and described their experiences on that day. One witness testified that when he arrived at his polling station he was told that he was listed as a convicted felon, and eliminated from the list of eligible voters. He was only allowed to vote after he challenged the information, which was double-checked by election officials and found to be incorrect.

Another person testified that she felt intimidated by a heavy police presence at her polling station. There had been five police cars that lined up in the area and formed a roadblock. Predictably, the police denied the charges and said that roadblocks were set up for the purposes of establishing security and controlling the flow of traffic.

And when testifying before the commission, 'Brother Gov' Jeb Bush denied any involvement in the alleged voting irregularities. He stated that he first became aware of problems the day *after* the election, and that he was looking to update the voting equipment for future elections. He also claimed to welcome the committee's inquiry into the election process, and said that he was not aware of any deliberate attempts to deny people their right to vote.

He added that he hoped that the commission would, "sort out any of the discrepancies that might exist, so that we can work together to build a world-class election system for Floridians that might be a model to the rest of the country." He also said that he had appointed a task force to look into charges like those reported by several witnesses who testified before the commission.

Finally, he told the committee that he had recused himself from direct involvement with the election because George Bush was his brother. He clearly implied that he had been totally hands off, was uninvolved in the planning that went into pulling off the theft of the election, and was unaware that thousands of Floridians had their rights violated.

All along he never did the very thing that individuals typically do when they feel that they are unfairly charged with misdeeds – he never refuted the evidence.

How 'Brother Gov' was able to sit before the committee and keep a straight face without laughing hysterically I'll never know. And I can only imagine how much fun the Bush Brothers must have had whenever they spoke to each other about the games played in Florida.

Next up in front of the commission was 'Kathy the Kleptomaniac' Harris.

Harris told the commission, "From the time that we entered the recount period I wanted to follow the law" when referring to the direction of the U. S. Supreme Court to stop the process.

Excuse me, but what happened to following the law before and during the election process? What an incredible statement for her to make in light of everything that had happened.

And rather than admitting that thousands of Floridians had illegally been denied the right to vote, just like 'Brother Gov' she played the 'we should let the past stay in the past and focus on the future' game. And like 'Brother Gov', she blamed the errors on the voting technology.

Harris said that she believed that the most important issue that could be addressed moving forward was the voting systems. "We want to make sure that the will of every voter is self evident and we think that they will not only be able to feel comfortable with that, but that we can be assured" she told the commission.

And then, just like 'Brother Gov' did, she attempted to distance herself from the management and oversight of the election process.

She told the commission that although, as the secretary of state, she was responsible for the oversight of the voting process there was a subordinate who handled the day-to-day issues, and that there were many things that she was only made aware of when a decision was required.

What a joke. The committee and the world was to believe that the same person who happened to be Florida's Secretary of State, co-chairman of the Bush presidential election committee, *and* a member of the State Board of Canvassers was *only* made aware of what was going on if there were issues to be addressed.

The tone and content of the testimonies of 'Brother Gov' and 'Kathy the Kleptomaniac' were almost identical; despicably identical. The commission was simply given the old 'we promise to do better next time' routine.

Mary Frances Berry, the commission's chairwoman, stated, "We know that in elections across the country there will be from time to time irregularities. But these should be the exceptions, not the rule...We know that something happened here. Something very wrong happened to some people. We still don't know its dimensions, or who is responsible or what should be done about it."

She also stated that the commission believed that 'Brother Gov' had some responsibility for what took place. She said, "While Harris and the county supervisors of elections played major roles in the administration of the election, Governor Bush is the glue that holds all these things together."

The glue that held all these things together? He was more like the venom that poisoned the process for many honest Floridians.

And on March 9, 2001 Chairperson Berry issued a statement regarding the commission's preliminary report that was very critical of the manner in which the Florida election had been conducted. It indicated that the commission was very interested in keeping informed as to the improvements that were planned for implementation in the voting system.

The investigation found several problems, including poor and dysfunctional equipment in polling stations located in rural and poor communities, errors in the process by which people were determined to be ineligible to vote, and the inappropriate use of police at and near select polling stations.

From the standpoint of charges that blacks were disproportionately affected by voter fraud, she stated that the evidence from the investigation might have ultimately *supported* findings of discrimination. The commission was attempting to document whether, and if so, how long state, county, and local officials knew that these differences might have impacted blacks in particular as well as other minority groups.

Ultimately, the commission released a final report in the following June that concluded that the manner in which the presidential election was conducted in Florida unjustly penalized minorities. The report stated that there was unequal access to modern voting equipment, and that the state made 'overzealous efforts' to remove voters from the voting eligibility, and that this had the greatest *negative* impact on black Floridians who had a legal right to vote.

If the Civil Rights Commission could analyze the facts and come to this conclusion, why couldn't the U.S. Supreme Court? The answer, simply put, is that it wasn't in the court's political best interest to do so.

But all of this was too little and too late. Whatever its findings, the commission did not have the power to change the election results. It could only recommend voting reforms to the Congress or pass evidence of wrongdoing onto the Justice Department.

So the first of many other Bush family 'coincidences' to come was now water under the bridge.

Unfortunately, the theft of the Florida election, and the ultimate Bush takeover of the White House, would prove to have significant and dire consequences for this country.

Chapter 12

The Bush Family's War

The attack on America on September 11th 2001 led to one of the most extensive manhunts ever around the world. Bush immediately spoke about leading a crusade to capture Osama bin Laden in Afghanistan, and to bring him to justice before the American people. I was and continue to be supportive of this objective. The al Qaeda faction has proven to be a major threat to international security.

However, somewhere along the way the story changed, and we were sold a war against *Iraq!* We had been attacked by *Afghanistan*-based al Qaeda, and our response was to attack *Iraq.* Fifteen of the nineteen hijackers were from Saudi Arabia, and we were attacking Iraq.

America had never been as much as threatened by Iraq but it was the target.

And how was this positioning achieved?

It was achieved by playing on the strong emotions of the American people. We had just been attacked, and our emotions and sympathies were ripe for exploitation.

But what was Bush's real motivation?

Have you ever heard of the Hatfields and the McCoys, the original feuding families of American folklore who hated each other? America's *reality* is that a Bush-Saddam Hussein family feud is precisely what got us into the Iraq War. This war has resulted in the death or injury of thousands, with no reasonable end in sight to American troops living in danger or losing their lives in Iraq.

99

Bush would have liked us to believe that the family feud played no part in the initiation of this war. But at this point he had an honesty and credibility problem. If you can steal a democratic election with a straight face, it's hard to be given the benefit of the doubt where this war is concerned.

Sorry, but I tend not to trust thieves easily.

The simplest way to make the point is to go through a chronology of actual *facts* and *quotes* made publicly regarding our history with Iraq (accompanied by my commentary of course). This is a history that goes back to Former President George Bush Sr. (I can call him president since he legitimately won *his* election), his history in the oil industry, and the politics leading up to the Persian Gulf War between Iraq and Kuwait that began in 1990. That war was the birth of the Bush-Hussein Family Feud.

George Bush Sr. and the Oil Industry

When George Bush Sr. graduated from Yale University in 1948, he decided to move to Texas and start a career in the oil industry. In 1953, after a few years of learning the business, he formed an independent oil company with a group of partners in the town of Midland. The partnership went by the name of the Zapata Petroleum Group. George Bush Sr. was very successful in building the company through his ability to locate and acquire high potential land, and have it drilled for oil at a cost that would make the venture quite profitable.

The partnership ended a year later, and Bush Sr. assumed the offshore oil services division of the business under the name of the Zapata Off-Shore Company. He got involved in developing offshore drilling around the world, and in the process became very well educated about foreign competition, and the impact that it could have on the price of oil in the U.S. At that time oil reserves had been built up in the Middle East, and the flow of oil into the U.S. was controlled by quotas imposed by President Eisenhower. These quotas were in place in order to control the balance between imported oil and domestic production, which was important to the U.S. economy.

In the mid 1960's, Bush Sr., whose father Prescott was a former Senator from Connecticut, decided to leave the business world and enter politics. He eventually became a Congressman, and his main constituents were the Texas oil producers. After serving in Congress, Bush Sr. moved on to several high-level government positions, including the head of the Central Intelligence Agency (CIA).

In 1980, after an unsuccessful run against Ronald Reagan for the presidency in the Republican primary, Bush Sr. was selected by Reagan to be his Vice President. Reagan strongly believed that the international 'free market' should drive the energy industry, so he moved to de-regulate oil prices. Subsequently, in 1986 the cost of oil from the Middle East dropped significantly, which led to a fear in the U.S. that the domestic oil industry would have been devastated because cheaper oil from the Middle East would have flooded the country.

In 1986, Bush Sr. took a trip to Saudi Arabia to show U.S. support for the region during the Iran-Iraq War. While on this trip he attempted to address his concern that Saudi Arabian oil prices were at a very low level, which had a negative impact on U.S. based oil producers. Clearly a part of his motivation was to soften the impact that cheap Middle Eastern oil was having on his constituents in Texas, where there was a significant loss of business and jobs attributed to the importation of oil. Bush Sr. was quoted as saying that he would try hard to persuade Saudi Arabia to address oil prices in the interests of the American economy and national security. Bush Sr. said, "I think that it is essential that we talk about stability, and that we not just have a continued free fall like a parachutist jumping out without a parachute."

Bush's personal objective was to have Saudi Arabian oil prices *raised* in order to benefit the American market. During his trip he indicated to Saudi Arabian officials that if prices continued to remain too low the U.S. Congress would have to put a tariff on oil imports. He said, "I know I'm correct. Some things you're sure of. This I'm absolutely sure of - that low prices would cripple the domestic American energy industries, with serious consequences for the nation."

By taking the position that Saudi Arabia should adjust its oil prices to favor U.S. domestic interests, Bush found himself in direct conflict with the Reagan administration's policy of letting the free market determine pricing. When he was asked about this conflict he responded, "I don't know that I'm defending the oil industry. What I'm doing is defending a position that I feel very, very strongly... whether that's a help politically or whether it proves a detriment politically I couldn't care less."

The Saudi Arabian government took Bush seriously, and because they relied on the U. S. in part for their own security they were motivated to address his concerns. This ultimately led to the Organization of Petroleum Exporting Countries (OPEC) raising oil prices in the Middle East to a level that was advantageous to the U.S. economy and satisfactory to the OPEC nations.

In 1988, Bush Sr. succeeded Reagan as U.S. President, and at the time oil prices were relatively low and there were plentiful reserves around the world. However, he wasn't comfortable with that situation because the Middle East had increased its reserves to a level where it controlled seventy percent of the world's oil supply. The U.S. was importing oil at the highest volume in its history, and the world was becoming increasingly dependent on oil from the Persian Gulf. Fortunately, there was no oil crisis on the horizon at the time.

And then the Gulf War between Iraq and Kuwait began.

Kuwait had been governed as a part of the Ottoman province in southern Iraq until 1899 when the British government began to provide it with protection from Iraq.

In 1961, the British government granted Kuwait fully independent status. Shortly thereafter, Iraq resumed its historical claim that Kuwait was rightfully Iraqi territory.

In 1963, after years of being unsuccessful in its attempts to reclaim Kuwait, Iraq finally recognized Kuwait as being independent. However, the relationship between the two countries remained tense, and there were occasional clashes between them along the Iraqi-Kuwaiti border.

The relationship improved during the war between Iran and Iraq (which was fought from 1980-1988), largely because Kuwait provided Iraq with military assistance. However, after the war Iraq fell $80 billion in debt as a result of the cost of its reconstruction, and demanded that Kuwait agree to forgive its share of the war debt.

Iraq also claimed that Kuwait was pumping oil from a field along the Iraqi-Kuwaiti border without sharing the revenues, and accused Kuwait of producing more oil than was allowed under quotas set by the OPEC. This alleged practice depressed the price of Iraqi oil, which was their primary export.

Consequently, Iraq became increasingly agitated and began to mobilize troops on the Iraqi-Kuwaiti border early in the summer of 1990.

In August 1990, Iraqi forces attacked and occupied Kuwait. During the following few weeks, the United States and other countries sent six hundred thousand troops to neighboring Saudi Arabia in an attempt to prevent further Iraqi occupation, and possibly drive Iraqi troops out of Kuwait.

January 16, 1991 – After diplomatic efforts to end the Iraqi-Kuwaiti War proved unsuccessful, the U.S. led an international coalition in a war against Iraq. Many

103

Americans were opposed to the war, arguing that the only reason for U.S. involvement in the conflict was to guarantee a cheap supply of oil.

The war ultimately ended just six weeks later on February 27, 1991.

Many Americans believed that, as an alternative to going to war, economic sanctions could have been used effectively against Iraq. However, former President George Bush Sr. took the position publicly that U.S. involvement was about 'principle' and not oil, and that economic sanctions would not have worked.

About principle? Not oil? I guess that George Sr. thought that the average American wasn't very bright.

Bush Sr.'s concern was that if Iraq's Saddam Hussein was able to capture Kuwait, Hussein's next step would have been to invade Saudi Arabia and attempt to take over its oil fields. And if Hussein was successful in taking over Kuwait, he would have had control over twenty percent of OPEC's production and twenty-five percent of the total oil reserves around the world! Iraq was not an ally of this country, so the risk of it having significant power in the region was dangerous to our interests.

That's why Bush Sr. sent U.S. troops into the Gulf War.

So after first standing on 'principle' Bush Sr. was quoted as saying, "Our jobs, our way of life, our own freedom and the freedom of friendly countries around the world would all suffer if control of the world's great oil reserves fell into the hands of Saddam Hussein."

Was the truth so hard?

Two and a half years later the bad relationship between the two countries got worse. Much worse.

In 1993, under President Clinton, the U.S. government uncovered evidence that Bush Sr. had been the target of a Saddam Hussein-led assassination plot. Hussein's desire to assassinate Bush Sr. was driven by the actions that Bush had taken in leading forces that drove Iraqi soldiers from

Kuwait in the Persian Gulf War. Hussein was firmly believed to have been behind the assassination plot, and was attributed by the CIA as having said in the Iraqi media that he would hunt Bush Sr. down and punish him, even when he was out of office.

The plot, which was designed by the Iraqi Intelligence Service, was for Bush Sr. to be the victim of a car bombing attack during his visit to Kuwait in April 1993. The evidence for the plot consisted of two related pieces of information.

U.S. intelligence officials found a one hundred and seventy-five pound car bomb in Kuwait City. An analysis performed by Federal Bureau of Investigation (FBI) bomb experts found conclusive evidence that it was linked to the Iraqi Intelligence Service. Specifically, there were several key components of the bomb that were overwhelmingly consistent with the components of bombs previously constructed in Iraq.

In addition, the U.S. government had credible confessions from two leaders of a group that was given the task of carrying out the assassination. According to those suspects, they met with parties that they believed were associated with the Iraqi Intelligence Service regarding the details of the assassination plot.

The suspects were also given a vehicle loaded with hidden explosives, and were told to drive to Kuwait University where Bush Sr. was going to be honored for the role that he played in ending the Persian Gulf War. The suspects said that their vehicle was to be parked near the motorcade route, and to be detonated from a point several hundred feet away when Bush's vehicle was in range. The bomb was believed to be deadly for a distance of up to a quarter of a mile.

The FBI was also told that if the bomb failed to detonate via remote control, the back-up plan was to detonate it with a timing device planted on a street in Kuwait City.

105

On June 26, 1993, in retaliation for this assassination plot, the U.S. launched twenty-three Tomahawk missiles targeted to the Iraqi Intelligence Service's headquarters in Baghdad. The missiles struck the building late that night in an attempt to minimize the potential of killing innocent Iraqis. They were programmed to hit strategic locations in the building that would ruin the capability of it being used by the Iraqi government, and were successful in doing so.

Following the bombing, Iraq was warned that any attempt to retaliate would be met with swift and powerful force.

And three years later…

January 16, 1996 – On the fifth anniversary of the beginning of the Gulf War, former President George Bush Sr., in an interview with broadcaster David Frost regarding the outcome of the war stated, "I think that maybe in retrospect we could have done more. The ending wasn't quite as clean as it might have been if Saddam Hussein had come to the tent, laid down his sword, and left office."

Bush suggested that the U.S. led coalition did not have a legal mandate to assassinate Hussein or overthrow his regime. However, Bush Sr. said he would not have minded if Hussein had been killed in the war. "Saddam Hussein was the commander-in-chief of the Iraqi forces," he said, "and if his life had been snuffed out in a bombing attack or something, too bad. That's one of the prices of war."

Bush Sr. also said, "Hussein was a wacko." He added that he would have risked impeachment to go forward with military action against Iraq even if the Congress had not approved it. "I know I would have gone forward against Saddam" Bush Sr. said, "I expected that impeachment papers would have been filed immediately if we'd gone into battle without sanction by the Congress."

Sounds personal to me. Saddam Hussein snuffed out in 'a bombing attack or something, too bad?' This was personal. But how else would he have been expected to feel about an individual who planned to kill him in cold blood?

He also said that he disliked Hussein so much that he would have disregarded the Congress if they had not supported him, and risked impeachment to go after him. And that would have taken place *before* the assassination plot was discovered a few years later.

When you think about it, how many presidents would do anything in full view of the Congress and the American public that could lead to even the consideration of impeachment unless they were more than angry? (Richard Nixon's and Bill Clinton's battles with the impeachment process don't count - these Presidents thought that their little indiscretions would be kept secret).

Former President Bush Sr. had grown to hate Hussein because Hussein posed the greatest international threat to his power during his presidency, and showed a total disregard for U.S. interests in the Middle East. Hussein was antagonistic toward Bush Sr., and attempted to build his power in the Middle East in spite of the objections of the U.S. and other countries.

In addition, Hussein posed a threat to Bush Sr.'s status with his constituents in the oil industry. Going back to the 1950's and 1960's when he was first in the oil business before moving into the political arena, Bush's power base was oil money and Hussein was looking to undermine that power base.

Then came the kicker. Hussein planned to kill him!

I wonder if his son knew this fact. What's your guess?

A few years later, George Bush Jr. stole (as opposed to being democratically *elected* to) the presidency, and was inaugurated in January 2001. Eight months later the 9/11 attack on America took place.

Help Me, Cheney, Rumsfeld, Powell, and Rice - How Do I Sell A War With Iraq?

George Bush Jr. was now in the chair once occupied by his father, and had his chance to escalate the Family Feud. Here are the events that led up to the Iraq war.

January 29, 2002 - In Bush's first State of the Union Address he named North Korea, Iran and Iraq as an "axis of evil", and said that indifference to them could be "catastrophic". He also warned that America could not wait in addressing terrorist threats: "Time is not on our side. I will not wait on events while dangers gather. I will not stand by as peril draws closer and closer."

It sounds like a pre-emptive strike was in the making. But who was the target?

June 1, 2002 - While addressing the graduating class of the West Point Military Academy Bush said, "Containment is not possible when unbalanced dictators with weapons of mass destruction can deliver those weapons on missiles or secretly provide them to terrorist allies... We have our best chance, since the rise of the nation state in the 17th century, to build a world where the great powers compete in peace instead of prepare for a war...America has, and intends to keep, military strengths beyond challenge, thereby making the destabilizing arms races of other eras pointless, and limiting rivalries to trade and other pursuits of peace."

Bush's pre-emptive strike philosophy hadn't changed, and he needed a reason for moving his agenda forward.

Let's see, how about using concerns about weapons of mass destruction (WMD's)? What a great rallying point. Surely no one could have an issue with stopping uncontainable dictators harboring WMD's!

And besides, the American public was with him, especially after 9/11. We were angry and we didn't know where Osama bin Laden (the alleged mastermind of the attack) was, but somebody had to pay!

September 12, 2002 - Bush addressed the United Nations (U.N.), calling on it to move quickly to enforce its resolutions demanding that Iraq disarm its weaponry. He said, "The purposes of the United States should not be doubted. The Security Council resolutions will be enforced. The just demands of peace and security will be met - or action will be unavoidable, and a regime that has lost its legitimacy (Iraq) will also lose its power."

Bush continued, "Iraq has answered a decade of U.N. demands with a decade of defiance...All the world now faces a test, and the United Nations [faces] a difficult and defining moment...Are Security Council resolutions to be honored and enforced or cast aside without consequence? Will the United Nations serve the purpose of its founding, or will it be irrelevant? By evading U.N. sanctions and frustrating arms inspections since the 1991 Persian Gulf War, Saddam poses exactly the kind of aggressive threat the United Nations was born to confront."

Iraq? Saddam Hussein?

Of all of the potential targets to go after, the primary threat just happened to be Saddam Hussein? What about other countries with state-sponsored terrorism? What about Libya, Syria, or Iran?

There certainly couldn't have been a personal vendetta involved here, right? Are we to believe that Iraq being Bush's primary target was just a simple 'coincidence' and unrelated to his father's history with Hussein? This Bush family is just full of coincidences - just like the Florida election coincidence involving his Brother Jeb.

Here's the critical question. Wasn't America's objective after 9/11 to find Osama bin Laden? How did Bush go from bin Laden to Hussein? All of this couldn't have been an excuse to justify going after the Bush family's archrival, could it? I can't imagine anyone going that far. He wouldn't have stooped as low as to drag the country into a war against a dictator who did not attack us on 9/11 for his own personal reasons, would he? But the country was emotionally positioned for war, wasn't it?

And what specific information did he have in order to justify going after Iraq to America and the rest of the world? Why, WMD's of course! Who would question going after Iraq's WMD's?

So Bush argued that Hussein had continually violated U.N. demands for disarmament, and had spit in the U.N.'s eye. His issue wasn't personal with Hussein, he was simply mad about how the U.N. had been treated!

In spite of Bush's position, France and Russia, two of the five permanent members of the U.N. Security Council with the power to veto a resolution in favor of a U.S. attack on Iraq, supported conducting thorough weapons inspections instead. They did not support a war. At that time, only Britain supported the U.S.

In the same session U.N. Secretary-General Kofi Annan told the General Assembly, "No nation should act alone as a matter of political convenience."

But this is America. Whether the U.N. agreed or not, Bush was going to do what he wanted to do. The U.S. would conquer. We knew better than the rest of the world.

We were attacked by one dictator, so the only logical thing to do was to go after another!

September 16, 2002 - Iraq said that it would allow international weapons inspectors to return to the country, and that it would be governed by the timetable established by the U.N. Security Council.

This wasn't good enough for Bush. He had already said that we know that Iraq had WMD's. Absolutely. Without question.

September 18, 2002 - Former President Bush Sr., in an interview with CNN's Paula Zahn, said he had "nothing but hatred" for Saddam Hussein, but he also had no regrets that during the Persian Gulf War the international coalition did not capture him. He also stated that he knew that the coalition would have ended if capturing Hussein was the issue. "My only regret is that I was wrong, as was every other leader, in thinking that Saddam Hussein would be gone... Now, am I happy Saddam Hussein is there? Absolutely not. But am I going to be moved by the Monday morning critics who now say we should have done it differently when they were totally silent back then? No."

He continued, "I *hate* Saddam Hussein. I don't hate a lot of people. I don't hate easily, but I think his word is no good, and that he's a brute. He's used poison on his own people. There's nothing redeeming about this man. I have nothing but *hatred* in my heart for him. But he's got a lot of problems, and immortality isn't one of them."

Gee, Bush *Jr.* told the U.N. that going after Iraq was a military necessity, and just six days later his father strongly stated, "I hate Saddam Hussein...I have nothing but hatred in my heart for him," adding that, "Immortality wasn't one of Hussein's problems." Sounds like a death threat to me.

All of this was too closely connected between father and son for me to believe that there wasn't a family issue here.

September 26, 2002 - During a Republican fundraiser in Texas Bush, when speaking about Hussein stated, "There's no doubt his hatred is mainly directed at us. There's no doubt he can't stand us...After all, this is the guy that tried to kill my dad at one time."

I guess the cat got out of the bag for a moment. There aren't too many people who wouldn't want to go after someone who tried to 'kill their dad'. And for Bush to specifically mention his dad, as opposed to the good of the country, as his sole motivation for going after Hussein is particularly telling.

Without a doubt, targeting Iraq was personal, and had nothing to do with the country's best interest.

Early October 2002 - The U.S. and Britain were in the process of drafting a U.N. resolution that would have given Iraq approximately two months to fully cooperate with weapons inspectors, and given the U.N. broad powers to hunt for suspected WMD's. Under the potential resolution, if Iraq failed to comply with the terms or disclose the required information within thirty days, it would have been subject to a military attack.

October 10, 2002 - Congress adopted a joint resolution authorizing the use of force against Iraq. The House of Representatives voted 296 to 133, and the Senate voted 77 to 23 to allow Bush to use military force against the alleged threat posed by Iraq.

That was a great day for the Bush Family! Now the legislature was on the team.

October 11, 2002 - The Pentagon ordered the Army and Marines to deploy staff to Kuwait in anticipation of military action against Iraq.

Bush didn't want to wait too long to start the deployment process. I guess that he couldn't afford to wait with all of those WMD's sitting over there!

October 23, 2002 - The U.S. introduced a draft resolution on Iraqi disarmament to the U.N. Security Council. The draft resolution said that Iraq was to provide inspectors with immediate and unrestricted access to any sites in the country, including presidential sites. It also stated that any interference in the process must be reported to the council.

Bush had our country in his pocket. If only he could have had the U.N. in his other pocket, he would have owned the world!

November 8, 2002 - The U.N. Security Council unanimously adopted a revised U.S. draft resolution to send U.N. weapons inspectors back to Iraq. Iraq was given seven days to accept the resolution. It called for Iraq to declare the WMD's that it had in its possession within thirty days, and give weapons inspectors unrestricted access to the country for forty-five days. The inspectors then had until January 24, 2003 to report their findings to the Security Council.

This must have been a tough day for Bush. Everything was being lined up to fire the first shot in the second round of the family feud, and now the U.N. had forced the issue, which led to a revised U.S. draft resolution. It was dragging out the process by supporting some inspections program, and calling on some crazy notion called diplomacy.

Oh well.

December 2002 - January 2003 - Troops and equipment were deployed to strategic positions in the Middle East.

What a twist of fate. The leader of the family feud, who wanted to go to war, got to be home for the holidays. Conversely, the military troops, who wanted to be home for the holidays, were shipped off to war. What's wrong with this picture?

January 28, 2003 - Bush said in his State of the Union address, "Twelve years ago, Saddam Hussein faced the prospect of being the last casualty in a war he started and lost. To spare himself, he agreed to disarm all weapons of mass destruction. For the next twelve years he systematically violated that agreement. Almost three months ago, the U.N. Security Council gave Saddam Hussein his final chance to disarm. He has shown utter contempt for the United Nations and the rest of the world."

Bush was still attempting to sell his plan to attack Iraq as having been motivated by Iraq's disregard for the U.N. I guess that the U.N. and the rest of the world were either too weak or too dumb to fend for themselves. Thank God Bush was the head of the free world.

He continued, "Our *intelligence* officials estimated that Saddam Hussein had the materials to produce as much as five hundred tons of Sarin, mustard and VX nerve agents. In such quantities, these chemical agents could also kill untold thousands. He's not accounted for these materials. He has given no evidence that he has destroyed them."

"U.S. *intelligence* indicates that Saddam Hussein had upwards of thirty thousand munitions capable of delivering chemical agents. Inspectors recently turned up sixteen of them - despite Iraq's recent declaration denying their existence...The International Atomic Energy Agency confirmed in the 1990's that Saddam Hussein had an advanced nuclear weapons development program."

"Our *intelligence* sources tell us that he has attempted to purchase high strength aluminum tubes suitable for nuclear weapons production...From *intelligence* sources we know, for instance, that thousands of Iraqi security personnel are at work hiding documents and materials from the U.N. inspectors, sanitizing inspection sites and monitoring the inspectors themselves...*Intelligence* sources indicate that Saddam Hussein has ordered that scientists who cooperate with U.N. inspectors in disarming Iraq will be killed, along with their families."

"With nuclear arms or a full arsenal of chemical and biological weapons, Saddam Hussein could resume his ambitions of conquest in the Middle East and create deadly havoc in that region. And this Congress and the American people must recognize another threat. Evidence from *intelligence* sources, secret communications, and statements by people now in custody reveal that Saddam Hussein aids and protects terrorists, including members of al Qaeda."

Ah, so the plot thickened. Bush had all of this information from his *'intelligence'* sources to conclude that Hussein was the world's greatest danger. He had lots of intelligence information, and the American people have always loved the ring of military intelligence. It has the exciting feel of espionage, and justifies the billions of tax dollars spent on intelligence initiatives.

And even better for Bush, all of this *'intelligence'* could possible have been sold as the basis for making a war with Hussein appear to be nothing personal. It was all about intelligence!

Bush also planted the seed in the minds of many Americans that Hussein was directly tied to 9/11 by mentioning him and 9/11 in the same sentence. The tactic was subtle but strong.

Bush continued, "Before September the 11th many in the world believed that Saddam Hussein could be contained. The world has waited twelve years for Iraq to disarm. America will not accept a serious and mounting threat to our country, and our friends and our allies. The United States will ask the U.N. Security Council to convene on February the 5th to consider the facts of Iraq's ongoing defiance of the world."

"Secretary of State Colin Powell will present information and *intelligence* about Iraqi's legal - Iraq's illegal weapons programs, its attempt to hide those weapons from inspectors, and its links to terrorist groups… We will consult. But let there be no misunderstanding: If Saddam Hussein does not fully disarm, for the safety of our people and for the peace of the world we will lead a coalition to disarm him."

"We seek peace. We strive for peace. And sometimes peace must be defended. A future lived at the mercy of terrible threats is no peace at all. If war is forced upon us, we will fight in a just cause and by any means - sparing, in every way we can, the innocent. And if war is forced upon us, we will fight with the full force and might of the United States military - and we will prevail."

'If war was forced upon us?' When did Hussein force war upon us? Was Bush inferring 9/11?

Absolutely. He was attempting to convince the American people that Saddam Hussein started a war with us, and that the U.S. had military intelligence that substantiated that we were vulnerable to more attacks from Hussein. And by now, Americans were ready to buy anything. Bush was on a real roll, and I bet that dad was enjoying the whole show.

But no speech is complete without throwing in a God reference. You know, the typical reference to our proud American history that makes us all want to run down to the Post Office and salute the flag while singing The Star Spangled Banner.

Bush continued, "Americans are resolute people who have risen to every test of our time. Adversity has revealed the character of our country, to the world and to ourselves. America is a strong nation, and honorable in the use of our strength. We exercise power without conquest, and we sacrifice for the liberty of strangers. Americans are a free people who know that freedom is the right of every person and the future of every nation. The liberty we prize is not America's gift to the world, it is God's gift to humanity."

We just love to immerse ourselves in self-compliments.

Let's see – 'adversity has revealed the character of our country'? We all know that based on history, certain groups in our society have historically faced and continue to face adversity. Surely Bush couldn't have meant all Americans.

And speaking of adversity, what adversity did *he* ever face - having to choose between Yale and another Ivy League school? Whether to keep or sell his partnership in the Texas Rangers major league baseball team? I have deep sympathy for Mr. Bush's personal adversities.

And how about 'Honorable in our use of strength, while exercising power without conquest and sacrificing for the liberty of strangers?' This was a coy set-up for the impending war. In other words, if we were to go to war against Iraq, it would have been because of our desire to sacrifice for the freedom of the Iraqi people. How philanthropic.

Like father, like son.

Then came, 'Americans are a free people who know that freedom is the right of every person.' Ironically, no reference was made to the fact that equal opportunity and treatment under the law is also supposed to be the right of every person.

Bush was saving that ending for a different speech.

And what about the right to vote in a democratic election, like the Florida election for example?

And finally the real tearjerker, 'The liberty we prize is not America's gift to the world, it is God's gift to humanity.' *God's* gift. If Bush went to war, he was carrying out God's will. He was a high-ranking servant of God. He not only had the blessing of God, but the power of God. The power to start a "pre-emptive war" against a country that had not been proven to have attacked us.

But most Americans will buy anything when God is attached to it. They'll even support the idea of killing a bunch of innocent people in a foreign country that did not initiate a conflict with us.

January 29, 2003 – Bush said that the removal of Iraqi President Saddam Hussein should be considered part of the war on terror, "Because of the nature of Saddam Hussein. He is a danger not only to countries in the region but, as I explained last night [in the State of the Union Address] because of his al Qaeda *connections*, because of his history, he is a danger to Americans…We're going to deal with him. We're going to deal with him before it's too late."

117

He also said that Saddam Hussein could use al Qaeda as a 'forward army' that could attack the U.S. with weapons of mass destruction and never leave a fingerprint behind. However, Iraqi Deputy Prime Minister Tariq Aziz told *Good Morning America* that, "Historically speaking, everyone in the region - everybody in the world - knows that Iraq has no connection with al Qaeda. We are quite different people, different in ideology, different in practice. And since the events of the 11th of September 'til now, this false accusation was repeated many times, and no evidence was presented."

Let's see. Not only did Bush know that Saddam Hussein had WMD's, but now he also knew that Hussein had a connection to Osama bin Laden and al Qaeda!! The case for a war was now even stronger! We had to get Hussein before it was too late.

Sure, Iraq's Deputy Prime Minister claimed that there was no connection to bin Laden and that the Iraqi people are different in ideology. But we are Americans, so to many of us all folks in the Middle East are the same. Many of us can't even differentiate between people from countries like China and Japan.

However, we sure know how to differentiate among ourselves.

February 2003 - The deployment of troops and equipment to the Middle East continued.

February 5, 2003 – Secretary of State Colin Powell addressed the U.N. in an attempt to make the case that Iraq was hiding WMD's. He presented the government's 'evidence' by using satellite photos illustrating alleged Iraqi efforts to move WMD's away from locations where weapons inspectors would most likely look. He also claimed to have had audiotapes of secretly recorded conversations among Iraqi officials. Powell said, "The information and intelligence that we have gathered point to an active and systematic effort on the part of the Iraqi regime to keep key materials and people from the inspectors in direct violation of (U.N.) Resolution 1441."

Who could possibly argue with solid proof? Actual pictures and audiotapes? Surely the U.N. would be motivated to support military action after seeing all that hard and irrefutable evidence!

March 16, 2003 – According to a USA TODAY/CNN/Gallup Poll, sixty percent (60%) of all Americans favored invading Iraq to remove Hussein from power. However, according to the same poll, the level of support dropped off if the United States, Britain and Spain failed to obtain the concurrence of the U.N.

In addition, if the U.N. Security Council formally rejected a resolution paving the way for military action, only fifty- four percent (54%) of Americans favored a U.S. invasion. And if the Bush administration did not seek a final U.N. Security Council vote, the support for a war dropped to forty-seven percent (47%).

The research also indicated that most Americans felt that Bush was doing a better job handling the Iraq situation than the U.N. was, and that France, Russia, and Germany were wrong to block a U.N. resolution authorizing a war.

In other words, roughly half of Americans did not want a war without U.N. Security Council support. Still, Bush was determined to go to war even if other countries and half of his own country's men and women were against it.

However, he had already managed to convince many Americans that the U.N. was weak and ineffective, and needed to follow his personal mandate from God. So, generally speaking, things were lining up nicely for him.

March 17, 2003 – France called for an emergency U.N. ministerial meeting to establish a timetable for Iraq's peaceful disarmament, despite a deadline set by the U.S and its allies for the U.N. to authorize war against Iraq. It appeared almost certain that a U.S.-led war would go forward without U.N. authorization because the fifteen-member council remained divided, and *no* acceptable compromise was on the table.

On the same day, Bush issued a forty-eight hour deadline to Hussein to leave Iraq by 8 P.M. Eastern Standard Time on March 19th. If Hussein failed to do so the U.S. and its allies were going to initiate military action against Iraq. In addition, the U.S. ordered all non-essential U.S. embassy personnel in Syria, Kuwait, and Israel to return to the United States within forty-eight hours.

This must have been like the night before Christmas!

March 19, 2003 - At 9:30 P.M. Eastern Standard Time the U.S. initiated a missile attack on Baghdad, the Iraqi capital city and the location of Saddam Hussein.

And so the war began...

Bush was to be congratulated. The family feud was officially on! I imagine that he and his dad got to toast his success in positioning the country for a war against Hussein.

Meanwhile, folks like me were still waiting to hear what we were doing about Osama bin Laden.

Unfortunately, the thousands of military personnel deployed to the Middle East were about to begin combat. These men and women were about to risk their collective lives for Bush's war. Regardless of the reason for their presence in Iraq, I firmly believe that they should be respected for their efforts. They were only doing what their government directed them to do.

March 20-27, 2003 - During week one of the war, the U.S. troops advanced toward Baghdad from the south, and moved within sixty miles of the city while battling resistance from the Iraqi militia. U.S. soldiers also parachuted into an area north of Baghdad in an attempt to secure the boundaries of the region.

March 28 - April 2, 2003 - U.S. ground troops advanced within thirty miles of Baghdad.

April 3, 2003 - U.S. troops attacked Baghdad International Airport as they moved within twelve miles of the city limits.

April 4, 2003 - U.S. troops captured Baghdad International Airport, and closed in on the city from the southeast. Meanwhile, in Washington D.C., the legislature passed an emergency bill authorizing $75 billion to pay for costs specific to the war, as well as anti-terrorism efforts internal to our country.

April 5, 2003 - U.S. troops entered Baghdad from the south, and had fighter planes conduct twenty-four hour missions over the city. U.S. officials claimed that the U.S. had captured more than fifty percent of Iraqi territory.

April 7, 2003 - U.S. troops surrounded at least one of Hussein's presidential palaces.

April 8-14, 2003 - U.S. troops took control of Baghdad, and began to seize control of surrounding cities, including Hussein's hometown of Tikrit. They were also challenged with policing Baghdad and other cities in an effort to bring looting and lawlessness under control.

During this timeframe Iraqis in central Baghdad toppled a huge statute of Hussein. This image became an international symbol of the fall of his regime.

April 15, 2003 - With the fall of Tikrit, the government declared that the major fighting was over in Iraq, and began withdrawing military troops and equipment. The focus of U.S. efforts switched to restoring order to the region, and eliminating the violence and looting in Iraq.

April 19, 2003 - Hidden cash was discovered in the walls of one of Hussein's palaces.

April 21, 2003 - The U.S. installed Paul Bremer, a retired U.S. General, as Iraq's new civil administrator. This action was deemed significant because it symbolized that order and control was being restored to the region.

121

And then came the big show...

May 1, 2003 – Bush made a dramatic landing aboard the aircraft carrier USS Lincoln, arriving in the co-pilot's seat of a Navy S-3B Viking after making two fly-bys of the carrier. The landing was covered live on television, and it was the first time that a sitting president had arrived on the deck of an aircraft carrier by plane.

Moments after the landing, Bush, wearing a green flight suit and holding a white helmet, got off the plane and saluted military personnel on the flight deck and shook their hands. Above him on the tower was a big sign that read 'Mission Accomplished'. "Great job," said Bush, "the battle of Iraq is one *victory* in a war on terror that began on September the 11th, 2001."

When asked if he took a turn piloting the plane, Bush said, "Yes, I flew it. Yeah, of course, I liked it." Then he posed for photographs with crew members, and looked up at the observation deck and held up both arms to the roar of the collective soldiers.

Wow, what a show! Bush swooped in on a military plane dressed like a fighter pilot - on live television no less. To me he looked like Alfred E. Newman from MAD Magazine in a space invader jumpsuit. To others, he was the great American hero. He acted as if combat was over and American soldiers were on their way home. Game. Set. Match.

For Bush, nothing could have beaten a superhero photo op. It was as if he had personally defeated Hussein and his regime. Just a little bit of ego, don't you think?

Chapter 13

Uh, Oh - The Story Is Starting To Unravel!

It's amazing how so much of what we were told by Bush when he was attempting to sell us the war was starting to fall apart. It started to appear that we were deceived with blatant lies and half-truths. But how could this be? We trusted Bush. He would never lie to us, would he? The Florida election was an act of thievery, not lying. And this was different than Florida, wasn't it?

Maybe the facts will continue to tell the story.
September 17, 2003 – Bush said that there had been *no evidence* that Iraq's Saddam Hussein was involved in the September 11, 2001 terror attacks, disavowing a link that had previously been suggested by his administration.

"No, we've had no evidence that Saddam Hussein was involved with September the 11th," said Bush.

No evidence that Hussein was connected to 9/11? Impossible. Bush had been so sure, and he had solid evidence. I was confused and disappointed. What happened to all of the evidence? He didn't exploit us did he?

I'm not the only person who was confused and disillusioned. An August 2003 Washington Post poll indicated that sixty-nine percent of Americans thought that it was likely that Hussein had a role in the 9/11 attacks.

They believed that a principal justification for the war against Iraq was a Hussein link to 9/11.

And by the way, there still weren't any WMD's found after six months of searching!

How would Bush and his team spin this one?

While acknowledging *no link* between Hussein and 9/11 Bush said, "There's no question that Saddam Hussein had al Qaeda ties."

Shortly thereafter Defense Secretary Donald Rumsfeld admitted that he had no reason to believe that Hussein played a role in the 9/11 attacks.

OK, so what was the big deal? Did Bush make an honest error by claiming that Hussein had a connection to 9/11? Or did we all mistakenly *infer* that he made that claim? In any case he still maintained that Hussein had a relationship with al Qaeda. That was his story, and he was sticking to it.

Then came Dick Cheney (I can't bring myself to call him vice president since he came along with Bush) who stated, "Some people, both in this nation and abroad, have questions about that strategy [to attack Iraq]...Make no mistake: [Bush] is acting to protect the American people against further attacks, even when that means moving aggressively against would be attackers."

Hussein went from being an accomplice in the 9/11 attacks to a 'would be attacker'. This was a major back-pedal on the part of the Bush administration, which was clearly caught in either a lie or a major web of deception.

September 22, 2003 - The Bush administration asked the legislature for an additional $87 billion to pay for occupying and rebuilding Iraq, as well as for the reconstruction of Afghanistan. The Senate Foreign Relations Committee took the position that, "There need to be a lot of questions asked - where is the $87 billion going? We didn't ask these questions when we passed the $75 billion supplemental bill. America needs to have those questions asked, and we deserve to know."

It goes without saying that the Senate and the legislature were fully complicit in the original deception along with Bush. But when the price tag became too steep, and there appeared to be no end in sight to the U.S. presence and casualties in Iraq, suddenly the legislators became Bush's 'poor little victims' who simply had not asked enough questions. This was a clear attempt on the part of legislators to save face with the American public who hadn't anticipated the human and financial price tag.

Don't we elect our politicians to ask the tough questions? Theoretically yes. But they were apparently caught up in the 'we've got to go after somebody' fever that the Bush administration had as well.

After Bush stood on the USS Lincoln and declared victory, many Americans probably thought the only remaining expense was the cost of transportation to bring the troops home. I guess that they were sadly mistaken.

September 23, 2003 - Bush told the U.N. that the transition to a democratic government in Iraq should not be hurried. He also said that the U.S. was working on a resolution that would, "Expand the U.N.'s role in Iraq." He added, "As in the aftermath of other conflicts, the United Nations should assist in developing a constitution, training civil servants, and conducting free and fair elections." He also said that the timeframe for handing over power to Iraqi should have been, "neither hurried nor delayed by the wishes of other parties."

Once again, Bush had an assignment in mind for the U.N. Assembly. I guess he thought that they needed to be told how they should have acted regarding his war, and would have appreciated his mentoring. He probably thought that they would have softened their position regarding his pre-emptive strike on Iraq, and may have given him money and military personnel to help offset the level of casualties experienced by the U.S., as well as the effects of the cost of the war on the mounting federal debt.

He was wrong.

U.N. Secretary-General Kofi Annan stated that pre-emptive strikes, "could set precedents that result in a proliferation of the unilateral and lawless use of force, with or without credible justification."

And French President Jacques Chirac took the position that the use of force should have only been approved by the U.N. Assembly. "No one should be able to accord himself the right to use force unilaterally and preventatively. In an open world, no one can isolate themselves, no one can act alone in the name of all, and no one can accept the anarchy of a society without rules. There is no alternative but the United Nations."

This was not a particularly good day for Bush.

October 22, 2003 - An internal White House memo from Defense Secretary Rumsfeld, regarding the Iraq War, was made public. In this memo, Rumsfeld said that the U.S. had no way of measuring progress in the war on terrorism, and was in for a long, hard slog in both Iraq and Afghanistan. He asked, "Are we winning or losing the global war on terror?...Is our current situation such that the harder we work, the behinder we get?" Rumsfeld said the war was extremely expensive, with the cost to the U.S. in the billions versus the cost to the terrorists in the millions.

Rumsfeld's memo also said that the U.S. should create a foundation aimed at tempering radical Islamic schools because, "they may be churning out new terrorists faster than the United States can kill or capture them."

Imagine that. The same guy who was always on television telling us how well the war against terrorism was going was telling his associates in private that he didn't know if we were winning the war, that it was too expensive, and that the terrorist organizations were creating terrorists faster than we could eliminate them! Which story were we to believe?

November 13, 2003 - Bush said that he wanted to see the plan for Iraqi self-rule be executed faster than originally anticipated. He suggested that a possible option would have been to shift power to the Iraqis before a formal constitution was put into place. According to national security advisor Condoleezza Rice, "What is important is that we find ways to accelerate the transfer of authority to the Iraqi people. They are clamoring for it. They are, we believe, ready for it. And they have very strong ideas about how that might be done."

This was yet another clever spin. Didn't Bush tell the U.N. less than two months prior that there would be no rush to turn over governance to the Iraqi people?

The U.S. had previously rejected a plan to hand over power to the Iraqi Governing Council until it had written a constitution, and held a democratic election. So what was the rush?

How about the fact that the world was witnessing the consistent death of U.S. troops and innocent Iraqis at the hands of the Iraqi insurgents?

How about the $160 billion and mounting price tag?

How about the fact that we had painted ourselves into a corner with little to no significant international military or political support?

How about the fact that we had no reasonable exit strategy whatsoever?

But Bush, then Cheney, then Powell, then Rumsfeld, and then Rice were telling us to believe that this position was being driven by the Iraqis.

January 20, 2004 - The U.S. appealed to the U.N. to assist in putting together a plan to accelerate the turnover of power to the Iraqi government, and establish the framework for a national election. U.N. Secretary-General Kofi Annan heard the appeal from the U.S., and agreed to send a U.N. team to Iraq to assess the potential for a national election. But the U.N. was clear: in order to maintain its independence in the conflict it was not going to establish an official presence in Iraq.

By now Bush was simply desperate for an exit strategy. The same person who couldn't get us into Iraq fast enough now couldn't get us out of Iraq fast enough!

He was not exactly the same guy flying the fighter plane onto the USS Lincoln in his Navy fighter suit, filled with bravado and claiming that the war in Iraq was over. Now he was groveling in front of the U.N. for help in getting the U.S. out of Iraq, the same U.N. that he told that he would go to war against Iraq with or without their support.

Did he really believe that the U.N. would go as far as to establish a presence in Iraq? It had pulled its staff out of the country following a suicide bombing that killed twenty-two people in its Iraqi headquarters during the previous August.

Help me understand. Was he really that detached from reality?

<u>January 20, 2004</u> - Bush gave his State of the Union address. With regard to the war he said, "America is on the offensive against the terrorists. Our greatest responsibility is the active defense of the American people." He also said that U.S.-led forces have engaged Iraq and Afghanistan in combat because "killers, joined by foreign terrorists, are a serious continuing danger. The men and women of Afghanistan are building a nation that is free and proud, and fighting terror. The work of building a new Iraq is hard, and it is right. And America has always been willing to do what it takes for what is right."

A few days later the second big lie was exposed...

January 24, 2004 - Former chief U.S. weapons inspector David Kay, who had quit his job after six months of leading the inspection team, announced his conclusion that Iraq did *not* possess either biological or chemical weapons!

Kay said, "I don't believe that they existed...What everyone was talking about is stockpiles produced after the end of the 1991 Gulf War, and I don't think there was a large scale production program in the 1990's...I think that we have found probably eighty-five percent of what we are going to find."

In addition, International Atomic Energy Agency chief Mohamed ElBaradei, the U.N.'s top nuclear expert said, "I am not surprised by this [conclusion]. We said already before the war that there was no evidence of this, so this is really not a surprise."

There was no evidence of WMD's in Iraq? No evidence? The alleged justification for the war against Iraq had no basis in fact? What about all of that military intelligence Bush referred to?

How much more did we need to hear before it became crystal clear what was going on? We had been clearly deceived by our government!

January 28, 2004 - David Kay testified before the Senate Armed Services Committee: "I believe it is time to begin the fundamental analysis of how we got here, what led us here, and what we need to do in order to ensure that we are equipped with the best possible intelligence as we face these issues in the future. Let me begin by saying we were almost all wrong, and I certainly include myself here."

I see. The best thinking was to go to war first, watch military personnel and innocent Iraqis get killed, and *then* closely examine whether military intelligence is accurate and reliable. What a great strategy!

The fact is that Bush was intent on going to war against Iraq whether or not the so-called intelligence was good, and the risk of closely examining the so-called intelligence

129

before the fact was that no justification may have been found for going to war in the first place.

But Bush had rolled the dice. If WMD's turned up, great. If not, he could blame the intelligence and make himself a victim who unwittingly acted on bad information!

Kay added, "We're also in a period in which we've had intelligence surprises in the proliferation area that go the other way. The case of Iran, a nuclear program that the Iranians admit was eighteen years - on that we under-estimated ...The Libyan program that was recently discovered was far more extensive than was assessed prior to that.

There's a long record here of being *wrong*. There's a good reason for it. Certainly proliferation is a hard thing to track, particularly in countries that deny easy and free access and don't have free and open societies...I do believe we have to understand why reality turned out to be different than expectations and estimates."

This was another significant point raised by David Kay. We underestimated Iran's nuclear program, and also discovered a program in Libya that was more extensive than was originally believed? These were intelligence surprises? Why didn't all of this information come to light *before* the war was initiated?

Is it possible that Bush knew this *before* attacking Iraq, and that if the public knew this information it would have been much harder to justify attacking Iraq as opposed to either Iran or Libya, if not Afghanistan?

January 30, 2004 - Condoleezza Rice told *Good Morning America* that Kay's findings, "raised questions that we will want to answer...It's too soon to consider an outside investigation because the search for weapons continues."

The administration needed to buy more time, and the way to do it was to claim it was too soon to know whether Kay was correct because the search for WMD's wasn't finished. If only they could sell the 'search continues' story to the American public until, oh, November 3, 2004, the day after the next presidential election.

February 2, 2004 - Bush announced that he would sign an executive order to initiate an investigation into the U.S. intelligence failures in Iraq. He said that he would name an independent, bipartisan commission to investigate the causes of faulty intelligence.

"I want all of the facts. We do know that Saddam Hussein had the intent and capabilities to cause great harm. We know he was a danger...he slaughtered thousands of people." Bush also said that the commission would, "Analyze where we stand, [and] what we can do better as we fight this war against terror."

Once again, he blamed all of this on intelligence.

Bush also got to choose the members of his commission.

Wouldn't it have seemed less suspect to have a commission with no direct ties to him or his spin team? With all that had happened, how could we possibly believe that the commission's findings and the timing of a report of those findings being made to the public would not be controlled by Bush?

Without a doubt, this independent commission was a smoke screen to cover his decision to go into Iraq, and to control the fallout from allegedly acting on 'bad intelligence'.

As for Hussein having slaughtered thousands of innocent people, no one would have argued that fact. What Bush failed to mention (a simple oversight I suppose), was that thousands more innocent people were slaughtered as a result of the war that *he* initiated!

February 5, 2004 - CIA Director George Tenet spoke at Georgetown University defending the U.S. intelligence estimate of WMD's in Iraq. He said, "The agency will never be completely right or wrong when the facts are in. Unfortunately, you rarely hear a patient, careful or thoughtful discussion of intelligence these days. But these times demand it, because the alternative, politicized and haphazard evaluation without the benefit of time and facts, may well result in an intelligence community that is damaged and a country that is more at risk."

I guess the spin team rehearsed its lines together.

Go to war first, and then have patient, careful and thoughtful discussion of intelligence, because these times demanded it.

We couldn't risk a damaged intelligence community? If you ask me the damage was already done!

Tenet said, "Analysts differed on several important aspects of these programs and these debates were spelled out in the estimate. They never said that there was an imminent threat. Rather, they painted an objective assessment for our policymakers of a brutal dictator who was continuing his efforts to deceive and build programs that might constantly surprise us and threaten our interests."

Something wasn't right here.

Didn't Bush say that we needed to take military action before it was too late? Doesn't that imply an imminent danger? Bush really felt an imminent danger although the CIA did not claim that there was an imminent danger? I'm really confused. Isn't it the CIA's responsibility for knowing what is going on?

Tenet said that U.S. intelligence sources had evidence to suggest that Hussein planned to restart his efforts to develop chemical, biological and nuclear weapons. He also claimed that U.N. inspectors were unable to fully account for Iraq's pre-1991 arsenal of weapons, and that intelligence gathered after inspectors left in 1998 suggested that Iraq was trying to conceal prohibited weapons.

"Together this information provided a solid basis on which to estimate whether Iraq did or did not have weapons of mass destruction and the means to deliver them." Tenet explained, "It is important to underline the word estimate, because not everything we analyze can be known to a standard of absolute proof."

When Bush was selling the war, he didn't estimate that Iraq had WMD's. He was certain about WMD's in Iraq. He didn't say 'everything cannot be known to a standard of proof.'

So now, hundreds of American fatalities and thousands of injuries later, Tenet was talking about estimates. Our government took the country into a pre-emptive war based on estimates. Not facts, but estimates. Bad estimates. And Americans were expected to be receptive to this explanation?

February 11, 2004 - Colin Powell told the House International Relations Committee that Hussein, "had to be dealt with, and [Bush] made the right decision. The dictator is no longer filling up mass graves or building up weapons of mass destruction."

In addition, Condoleezza Rice said, "Saddam was a dangerous man in the most dangerous part of the world. After 9/11, this president has borne a heavy burden to be certain that we are responding to threats and not simply allowing them to gather."

Poor Bush. He was carrying a heavy burden and was a victim of bad intelligence. How could we *not* feel sorry for him?

Rice continued, "The word of the United States in the United Nations, whose resolution we enforced, that word is finally good. And as a result of the fact that the word is now credible, we're getting movement on proliferation of weapons of mass destruction in other parts of the world, like Libya, where Colonel Gadhafi has voluntary decided to disarm his nation."

Yet another spin. How's this for logic at the highest levels of our government. In other words, going into Iraq with bad information was good because it led to Libya disarming.

We knew about Gadhafi's history for years, and David Kay said that Libya's program was much more extensive than originally believed. So why didn't we go after Libya as opposed to Iraq?

And when the case was being made to go to war, Bush did all of the talking. When he thought that the war was over he flew in grandiose style onto the USS Lincoln alone. Not with Tenet, Rice, Powell, or Rumsfeld. Alone. However, when the game was falling apart Bush wasn't front and center anymore. Now Tenet, Rice, Powell, and Rumsfeld were doing all of the talking. They were taking all of the tough questions. Why wasn't Bush front and center instead of hiding behind his staff?

April 2, 2004 - Colin Powell, on the trip home from Belgium after meeting with NATO, admitted that the case he presented to the U.N., which included claims that there were two specific trailers that were being used to make WMD's, may have been incorrect. He also said that the commission appointed by Bush to analyze the intelligence issues, "will look into these matters to see whether or not the intelligence agency had a basis for the confidence that they placed in the intelligence at that time. Now if the sources fell apart we need to find out how we've gotten ourselves into that position."

April 18, 2004 - Spain's newly elected Prime Minister, Jose Luis Rodriguez Zapatero, announced that he was withdrawing all Spanish troops from Iraq as quickly as possible. Zapatero promised the Spanish people that he would do so in part as a result of a commuter train bombing in Madrid. Al Qaeda claimed that the bombing was in retaliation for Spain's involvement in the Iraq War. In addition, Honduras also decided to remove its troops from the war. So much for the continued coalition support of the U.S. and Britain. And this happened shortly after it was made public that there were significant concerns about having adequate security in place for a new Iraqi government to be established.

Translation: U.S. troops would be in the Middle East for a long time.

At this point there has been too much double talking, finger pointing and rationalizing for me to keep up with. Quite honestly, the cover-up for the mess that this country was and continues to be in had fallen apart.

Try to follow this:

First we were told that we were going to hunt down Osama bin Laden and bring him to justice for the 9/11 attack. But we didn't.

Then we were told that Saddam Hussein was *involved* with al Qaeda in the 9/11 attack. And then he wasn't.

Then we were told that he was simply *tied to* Osama bin Laden. And then he wasn't.

Then we were told that Hussein had WMD's that put us in imminent danger. And then he didn't.

But we had military intelligence that backed Bush's claim. And then we didn't.

And we were sure that our legislators asked the tough questions before supporting the war. And then we were told that they hadn't.

And after going to war, we were told that we were winning the war on terrorism. And then we weren't.

And we understood that we had a viable exit strategy for Iraq. And then we didn't.

And we didn't need the support of the United Nations. But we did.

And all along President Bush was fully accountable. And then he wasn't.

And the CIA should have had the facts. But they didn't.

135

If the head of a company had this kind of a resume he or she would be fired on the spot. But this is politics, and too many Americans will allow a leader to get away with this track record because they would probably do the same thing if they were in charge, namely do the deed and hide behind excuses later.

There has always been a clear pattern of *deflecting blame* in the Bush family, and all of us are guilty of letting politicians like the Bush Brothers get away with it.

When Jeb Bush found himself squarely in the middle of the presidential election scandal in Florida, he blamed the problem on *bad technology*. Rather than ensure that all of the citizens of the state of Florida who had the right to vote were allowed to do so, he rigged the election just as he intended to, and then attempted to turn himself into a *victim* when the game was exposed.

When George Bush found himself squarely in the middle of the Iraq War scandal, he blamed the problem on *bad intelligence*. He set the stage to go to war against Iraq just as he had intended to, and then he attempted to turn himself into a *victim* when the game was exposed.

Rather than hold individuals like them accountable for manipulating the entire country, many Americans rally behind dishonest politicians because they've been led to believe that it's the patriotic thing to do. I believe that Bush knew this and took us into this war believing that he could explain away his actions as being a result of bad information. And the best way to string us along was to keep that facts out of the public eye as long as possible. So the game went on.

Couldn't someone out there tell us the truth??

Chapter 14

O'Neill, Clarke, and Woodward - What Is This All About?

I was just about to give up the hope of getting a straight and plausible answer about what was really behind going to war against Iraq. And for a while it appeared that being credible was synonymous with being a *former* employee of the Bush administration.

We know, for instance, that weapons inspector David Kay first resigned and then exposed what was truly going on with the Iraqi weapons inspection program and the state of U.S. military intelligence.

Then we heard from former Treasury Secretary Paul O'Neill and former White House counter terrorism chief Richard Clarke. O'Neill was fired by Bush after two years in his administration, in part because on several occasions he both publicly and privately took issue with Bush's tax policies. In January 2004, he conducted an interview with Lesley Stahl of *60 Minutes* regarding a book that he had written with author Ron Susskind.

According to O'Neill, during Bush's first National Security Council meeting, which took place *eight* full months before 9/11, "there was a conviction that Saddam Hussein was a bad person, and that he had to go. From the

137

very first instance it [Bush's focus] was about Iraq. It was about what we could do to change the regime. From day one, these things were laid and sealed. It was all about finding a way to do it. That was the tone of it. [Bush] was saying, 'go find me a way to do this.' For me, the notion of preemption - that the U.S. has the unilateral right to do whatever we decide to do - is really a huge leap."

O'Neill added that the discussion about Iraq continued in a National Security Council meeting two weeks later.

Ron Susskind stated that he acquired memos written during the first two months of the Bush administration that discussed an occupation of Iraq. They were specifically planning for a post-Hussein Iraq. In addition, Susskind acquired a Pentagon document written in March 2001 that included a map of potential areas for oil exploration in Iraq.

Clearly, David Kay, Paul O'Neill and Ron Susskind's accounts regarding Bush's pre-9/11 desire to specifically go after Saddam Hussein were very *consistent* with the chronology of facts related to the Iraqi War.

Predictably, the Bush administration's response was to attempt to discredit their reports and paint them as having no credibility. Imagine that - *Bush* calling these folks dishonest given his ever-changing story about the reason for going to war, and the manner in which he assumed the presidency in the first place.

But O'Neill was only one dissenting individual who had been in the Bush inner circle, so his singular account could be neutralized. That was until Richard Clarke came along to make things more difficult for the administration. Then there were two former White House officials with similar accounts.

Clarke, who also wrote a book about his White House experience, was interviewed by Leslie Stahl from *60 Minutes* in March 2004. He took serious issue with Bush's plan for running for re-election on his war record.

According to Clarke, on 9/11 Bush held meetings with senior officials regarding how to respond to the attack. Clarke stated that, "Rumsfeld was saying that we needed to bomb Iraq...and we all said no, no, al Qaeda is in *Afghanistan.* We need to bomb Afghanistan. And Rumsfeld said there aren't any good targets in Afghanistan, and there are lots of good targets in Iraq."

Clarke felt that Bush and Rumsfeld *wanted* to believe that Iraq was tied to al Qaeda. However, Clarke and George Tenet attempted to make the argument that there was *no* connection between Iraq and al Qaeda based on several years of investigation. Their feeling was that the military response should have been directed at Osama bin Laden and al Qaeda.

So what did Bush do?

According to Clarke, Bush took him into a room with a few other staff members, closed the door and directed him to find out whether Iraq was responsible for the attack. Clarke felt that Bush's tone was such that he was *expected* to come back with a report that said that Iraq was responsible. He told Bush that the matter had previously been assessed with an open mind, and that no connection could be found between Iraq and the attack.

Clarke stated, "He (Bush) came back at me and said 'Iraq. Saddam. Find out if there is a connection'; and in a very intimidating way. I mean [he meant] that we should come back with *that* answer. We wrote a report."

Subsequently, Clarke and the group took another serious look at the situation with participation from both CIA and FBI experts. They produced a report that went to the CIA leadership and then the FBI leadership for approval. "They all cleared the report," Clarke said, "and we sent it up to [Bush] and it got bounced by the national security advisor or deputy. It got bounced and sent back saying 'wrong answer...do it again.'"

139

Equally as disturbing, Clarke said that prior to 9/11 there wasn't a major concern about al Qaeda. He had attempted to engage senior administration officials in a serious dialogue regarding al Qaeda beginning in January 2001, and could not get a meeting until the following April. And that meeting was with the second in command in the appropriate government departments. Clarke began the meeting with the position that bin Laden and al Qaeda had to be dealt with. In response, Deputy Defense Secretary Paul Wolfowitz said that bin Laden was a 'little guy' and that *Iraq* needed to be the point of focus.

As usual, the Bush administration went into full defense mode. Joining the spin team was Stephen Hadley, second in command on the National Security Council.

According to Hadley, contrary to what Clarke asserted, Bush *did* take the potential threat of al Qaeda seriously before 9/11. "George Bush heard those warnings" said Hadley, "[Bush] met daily with George Tenet and his staff. They kept him informed and at one point [Bush] became somewhat impatient with us and said 'I'm tired of swatting flies. Where's my new strategy to eliminate al Qaeda?'"

Hadley claimed that all of the dialogue was about concerns regarding a potential al Qaeda attack overseas. He also said that Bush was concerned about whether there was the possibility of an attack in the U.S., and that he asked the intelligence community to look hard to ensure that nothing had been missed. Hadley also claimed that, "We cannot find evidence that this conversation between Mr. Clarke and George Bush ever occurred." When Leslie Stahl told him that *60 Minutes* had sources who confirmed the dialogue between Clarke and Bush, including an actual witness, he responded that he stood by what he said.

In April 2004, not long after the Richard Clarke interview, Bob Woodward, a highly credible and respected journalist, released a book that was written about the events leading up to the Iraq War. It was based on interviews with seventy-five top officials in the Bush administration, including Bush himself.

Woodward was interviewed by Mike Wallace from *60 Minutes*. In order to validate his book's assertions, Woodward allowed Wallace and his staff to listen to tape-recorded interviews and read transcripts to verify quotes from meetings with the key White House staff.

As it turned out, Bush was the only interviewee who allowed Woodward to quote him directly.

Woodward learned that just five days following 9/11, discussions began in Bush's office about going after Saddam Hussein after 'doing' Afghanistan first. According to Woodward, Donald Rumsfeld said, "This is an opportunity to take out Saddam Hussein, perhaps. We should consider it. Bush responded 'we won't do Iraq now. But it is a question we're gonna have to return to.'"

A few months later, after a November National Security Council meeting, Bush took Rumsfeld aside and asked him for the status of the war plan against Iraq. He also told Rumsfeld to keep the planning process a secret.

As a part of this secret plan, General Tommy Franks was directed to develop a war plan targeted at removing Saddam Hussein. And while he worked on the plan he denied every bit of the scheme in public.

On December 28th, Bush told reporters that he was "... focused on the military operations in Afghanistan" following a meeting that he had with his top aides and generals. And when asked about statements that he had made regarding 2002 being a year of war he addressed his concerns regarding *Osama bin Laden*. "Bin Laden and his cronies would like to harm America again" he said, "and would like to harm our allies. How do I know that? I receive intelligence reports on a daily basis that indicates that that's his desires."

The truth of the matter was that the meeting was principally focused on the preparations for a war against

141

Iraq. At the meeting, Franks presented his assumptions regarding the number of troops that would be required to fight a war, a commitment that Iraq would be given the priority for military resources, and the belief that fighting terrorism in Afghanistan and other countries would effectively divert attention away from Iraq.

The plan was developed over the next several months, and was estimated to cost in the neighborhood of seven hundred million dollars to execute. Bush approved the plan at the end of July 2002 without informing the Congress that it was even being developed.

And where did Bush get the money? He got it from an appropriation for the war in *Afghanistan* that had already been approved by Congress. Of course, this was unconstitutional because Congress had not approved that money for funding a war in Iraq. But the Florida election had already proved that abiding by the Constitution was not exactly a concern of his if it got in the way of his agenda.

The initial push for a war against Iraq was attributed to Dick Cheney, who had been the Secretary of Defense during the Persian Gulf War. He wanted to get Hussein, and pushed the case that Hussein had WMD's. A few weeks later, Bush went on public record claiming that 'a lot of people understand that he (Hussein) holds weapons of mass destruction.'

Then, according to Woodward, in December 2002 CIA Director Tenet made a presentation of his evidence regarding Iraq and WMD's. Bush said, "Nice try, but this isn't going to sell Joe Public. That isn't gonna convince Joe Public…this is the best we've got?"

By Bush's own admission, the evidence presented to him by the CIA did not support the position of going to war!

Given that fact, it's perfectly reasonable to expect that a responsible leader would have tempered his desires, and backed off of the notion of going to war, recognizing that there wasn't sufficient evidence to justify doing so.

Clearly, the decision to attack Iraq was made long before the facts were collected.

Ultimately, Bush declared war in early January 2003. He immediately told Rice, Rumsfeld, and Cheney about his decision, but chose to wait to notify Colin Powell separately. In his meeting with Powell he said, "Looks like war. I'm going to have to do this." Powell asked him if he was aware of the consequences. Bush responded that he understood the consequences, and knowing that Powell didn't want to go to war, asked Powell if he would be with him. Powell said that he was with Bush and would do the best job that he could.

An interesting fact in this scenario was that Bush did *not* consult with either Secretary of State Powell or Secretary of Defense Rumsfeld before going to war. Given the implications of going to war, it would logically follow that these individuals would have participated in the decision making process. Instead, he asked Rice, who had no war experience and, are you ready for this, Karen Hughes - his political communications advisor - for their input.

I guess a communications advisor would be an expert on the implications of initiating a war!

So the war began, and right at the outset our outstanding military *intelligence* sources kicked in.

The intelligence sources indicated that Hussein was going to be at a location by the name of Dora Farm, a family farm south of Baghdad. Based on this information, the first bombing attack in the war was on Dora Farm, and the administration began to believe that they got Hussein.

And surprise, surprise - they were wrong!

Woodward ended the *60 Minutes* interview by saying that Bush still believed that Hussein possessed WMD's, and that the war was absolutely the right thing to do. He added that Bush also believed that he (Bush) had a duty to free and liberate people.

143

A duty to free and liberate people. This sounds like the 'messenger of God' routine that we had heard from him before.

My bottom line question is: Who are *you* going to believe: Kay, O'Neill, Clarke, and Woodward; or Bush and the spin team?

We know that one team's story had consistently changed since the beginning of the war. This was the same team who claimed to have hard facts before the war and no facts after it began.

And just to seal the position, yet another White House insider, former Ambassador Joseph Wilson, came forward after having the dirtiest deed of the Bush administration done to his wife and him.

During Bush's 2003 State of the Union address, he claimed that he had credible information that Hussein had attempted to acquire a significant amount of uranium from Africa as a part of Iraq's alleged WMD proliferation program. However, Mr. Wilson had been to Africa in 2002 on behalf of the CIA and did not find one single piece of evidence to substantiate Bush's claim. Wilson went on record that he believed that the uranium claim and other assertions by the administration were fabricated in an attempt to make the case for going to war against Iraq.

Consequently, an unidentified person in the administration leaked to the press that Valerie Plame, Mr. Wilson's wife, was a CIA operative, in what appeared to be a deliberate attempt to destroy both of their careers.

Without question, this was done in an attempt to punish Mr. Wilson for his statements against Bush.

Ironically, about the only truthful revelation out of the Bush administration happened to be targeted to destroying people's careers. Maybe someday we will be told the truth about why we *really* went to war.

But I wouldn't hold my breath…

Chapter 15

Make Sure To Downplay The Casualties

The government has done a masterful job of desensitizing the American public to the impact of this war.

When the country was attacked on 9/11, we were provided with continual coverage of the most gruesome aspects of the crisis. We were constantly exposed to pictures depicting the loss of life, interviews with people directly involved in the events that took place on that day, and coverage regarding the hundreds of funerals, memorial services and other remembrances that took place around the country. We saw Bush in attendance at memorials, as well as at funerals and other 9/11 related activities.

I believe that the coverage was appropriate, and I shared in the tremendous sense of loss and devastation having lived through it first hand.

However, there has not nearly been the same kind of coverage regarding the loss of life and injuries suffered by American soldiers and civilians in Iraq. We haven't been exposed to the hundreds of funerals across the country for soldiers killed in combat, or heard from many of the families about the impact of the war on their lives.

145

We also haven't seen any real coverage regarding the thousands of military personnel who have suffered serious injuries. Many of these individuals lost limbs and sustained other serious injuries that have changed their lives forever.

I would bet that the vast majority of them went to war believing that our government at the very least had its facts straight about Iraq.

How many funerals has Bush appeared at before the national television cameras? How many stories have been broadcast with footage from the Walter Reed Army Medical Center in Washington D.C. regarding wounded soldiers? The answer is few to none.

And what about the thousands of innocent Iraqi citizens who have been killed or injured? These men, women and children have absolutely nothing to do with the Iraqi ruling regime. Our government has slaughtered people who were totally innocent of any violence against this country, or anyone else for that matter. We claim to abhor the slaughter of innocent Americans that took place on 9/11, but it appears we find the slaughter of innocent Iraqi citizens the right thing to do after 9/11.

I can only surmise that it's appropriate for the country to see in vivid detail the devastation we suffered when *we* were the victims of an act of war, but it's not appropriate to see the effects of war when we are the initiator.

In stark contrast, Spain, a U.S. ally in the Iraq War who provided thirteen hundred soldiers to help control activities in south-central Iraq, honored their casualties both formally and publicly.

On November 29th , 2003 seven Spanish intelligence agents were killed when attackers ambushed their vehicles with rocket propelled grenades and assault rifles.

Coffins bearing the seven agents were flown from Iraq to Madrid, Spain the following day. They were draped in Spain's flag and were carried from a military plane to hearses and driven to a military hospital to be autopsied. A ceremony, which was attended by Foreign Minister Ana Palacio and joint Deputy Prime Ministers Rodrigo Rato and Javier Arenas, was held on the Torrejon military base. At the ceremony Prime Minister Jose Maria Aznar declared a national day of mourning for the dead.

December 2nd was Spain's national day of mourning. The funerals were held at the National Intelligence Center, and were attended by Prime Minister Jose Maria Aznar, King Juan Carlos, and Queen Sofia. Flags flew at half-staff across the country, and the funerals were covered on state television. Eventually, the Spanish government decided to withdrawn its troops from the war.

I wonder when Bush is going to lead us in a national day of mourning.

We listen to the daily rhetoric coming from the White House about the various military operations in Iraq. Other than the prisoner abuse scandal at Abu Ghraib prison, these are the operations that they *want* us to see. But there are operations that our government will not profile for us. For example, there is one particular operation that I don't remember appearing in any of the coverage I have seen.

Have you ever heard of Camp Wolverine in Kuwait?

Camp Wolverine is home to the Theater Mortuary Evacuation Point where dead bodies are sent before being returned to U.S. When a body is recovered in Iraq, it is sent to a collection point and then flown to Camp Wolverine.

At Camp Wolverine, soldiers are responsible for transferring the bodies from body bags into metal coffins, and then inventorying the dead soldier's wounds and belongings. The findings are then documented, and the coffins are labeled for shipping. The coffins are packed with ice to preserve the bodies for embalming, and then shipped to Dover Air Force Base in Delaware.

So far the soldiers at Camp Wolverine have processed more than nine-hundred bodies and counting.

Americans might look at the war more critically if we were exposed to the details of what goes on in operations like Camp Wolverine. But the Bush administration has not seen fit to provide those details.

Instead, we are provided with just enough coverage to have a feel for what is really going on, and just enough information to avoid risking a significant emotional backlash from Americans.

I cannot imagine anyone finding this war and its repercussions remotely humorous. Especially Bush, who got us into this conflict. But apparently I'm wrong.

At the annual dinner for the Radio and Television News Correspondents Association, Bush showed photographs of himself acting like he is looking for something that he lost behind the furniture in the Oval Office.

"These weapons of mass destruction have got to be somewhere...nope, no weapons over there...maybe under here?" he joked.

As of the end of July 2004, more than nine hundred soldiers and seventeen thousand Iraqi citizens were killed. In addition, over twenty three thousand medical evacuations had taken place in Iraq. I would imagine that the families of the hundreds of soldiers who have been killed and the thousands of injured troops wouldn't share his humor. Neither would the families of the more than thirty journalists who lost their lives covering the war.

By the way, how many Bush family members were deployed to Iraq?

Chapter 16

Typical American Heroes

On March 23, 2003, Private First Class (Pfc.) Jessica Lynch, a 20-year-old woman from West Virginia, and her Army maintenance unit were ambushed in Iraq. Her unit, the 507th Maintenance Company, was a Patriot-missile maintenance crew from Fort Bliss, Texas, that was assigned to maintain military equipment. The unit was traveling in a convoy of eighteen high mobility multi-purpose wheeled vehicles (humvees), trailers and tow trucks on its way from Kuwait to Baghdad.

The trip was rerouted along the way, and their battalion commander did not verify that Jessica's unit was aware of the routing change. Consequently, it got separated from the battalion, made several wrong turns and ended up in the vicinity of the city of Nasiriyah. The unit attempted to retrace its steps, and wound up in the center of Nasiriyah. They were met by Iraqi forces that blocked its path and fired on the vehicles.

The first vehicle, the one that Lynch was traveling in, broke down. Subsequently, she got into a second humvee with several other soldiers, and they ultimately struck a jackknifed U.S. truck, killing or injury the other passengers. Lynch suffered serious injuries, including fractures to her spine that knocked her unconscious, as well as several bone fractures and a head injury. Her arms and legs were also crushed in the incident.

149

A total of eleven of her fellow soldiers were killed and five others were taken captive in the ambush, only to be freed several days later.

Pfc. Lynch was taken prisoner and held separately from her fellow soldiers for nine days.

Military sources in Iraq learned that she had first been taken to an Iraqi military hospital, and then transferred to Saddam Hussein General Hospital in Nasiriyah. The information that she was in Hussein General Hospital was provided by an Iraqi lawyer named Mohammed Odeh Rehaief who had visited his wife there.

According to Rehaief, a doctor told him about Lynch being in the hospital and, when it was unguarded by an officer, he sneaked into her room to see her. He subsequently left the hospital, found some Marines in Nasiriyah, and told them about having seen and spoken with Lynch.

At the request of the Marines, Rehaief went back to the hospital for information regarding access to the site, as well as an estimated count of the Iraqi troops inside the building.

Subsequently, a full scale rescue operation was conducted by a U.S. Special Operations Unit. When they entered the hospital they found that the Iraqi dissidents had left the facility, and that Iraqi doctors were treating Lynch. She was turned over to the American troops with total cooperation. There were no shots fired inside the hospital, and no one resisted her release.

The U.S. military filmed the rescue. American television aired the footage repeatedly, dramatizing how the special operations unit *captured* the hospital in the dead of night, and battled Iraqi troops on their way in and out of the facility.

The U.S. troops were also able to recover two American bodies from the morgue, and were directed to the graves of seven soldiers who were members of Pfc. Lynch's convoy.

Rahaief, his wife and daughter were granted political asylum in the United States in recognition of his contribution to the rescue.

Jessica Lynch's actual experience, however, turned out to be different than was reported by the U.S. officials and media, and the real facts ultimately surfaced.

The Real Story

U.S. officials in Iraq told the American media that during the ambush Lynch was stabbed and shot, and fired her M-16 weapon at several of her attackers killing them.

Actually, she had attempted to fire her weapon but it jammed. She did not kill any of her attackers, and she was neither stabbed nor shot.

I do not question the heroism and courage of Pfc. Lynch. She exhibited tremendous strength and resolve to survive the ordeal, and to begin the difficult process of recovering both physically and emotionally. When she returned to the U.S., she began a grueling physical therapy program after undergoing several medical procedures.

Lynch should be honored for her courage and the sacrifices that she made in the Iraq War.

She was also to be commended for coming out publicly and telling her true story for the public record, even though it was counter to the romantic version that the government wanted so much to hold on to. The government's version of what happened was typical of their recognition of 'select' heroes, regardless of the facts.

In an interview on *Primetime Thursday* in November 2003, Diane Sawyer asked Lynch about stories regarding the ambush. She addressed reports that claimed that during the ambush she was wounded by Iraqi gunfire, but kept firing until all of her ammunition was exhausted, shooting several of her assailants in the process.

151

Lynch said, "I'm not about to take credit for something I didn't do. I did not shoot, not a round, nothing. When we were told to lock and load, that's when my weapon jammed. I did not shoot a single round. I went down praying on my knees. That's the last thing I remember."

She also said that it hurt her to receive praise that she felt her colleagues deserved. Specifically, she was upset that people would make up stories that had no truth to them. She said that no one but her knew what happened during the ambush because the other passengers in the vehicle were all killed. She was the only person who could have told someone that she went down shooting.

Lynch continued, "But I didn't [go down shooting]. I did not...I don't look at myself as a hero. My heroes are Lori (Pfc. Lori Piestewa), the soldiers that are over there, the soldiers that were in the car beside me, the ones that came and rescued me."

Later in the interview she restated that her gun jammed, and that she was never able to defend herself or fire her weapon. She said Pfc. Piestewa may have been the one who went down firing, and that she wasn't taking credit for it.

"She [Lori] was there for me...She had my back the whole time," Lynch offered.

When she was asked if the military's dramatization of her rescue from the hospital bothered her, she stated that it did. She felt that she had been used as a symbolic hero and that what had occurred was wrong. She also couldn't understand why the rescue was filmed.

Talk about manipulation of the American people.

The government used Lynch for its own propaganda campaign. However, she had enough dignity to speak out. The ultimate act of hypocrisy is that the government would play up a rescue mission for the world to see, but when it comes to the casualties suffered day after day there isn't much sensational footage to be found.

I believe that Lynch deserved the media attention, and that more details should be made public about the experiences of significantly more of our soldiers. However, as usual the government chose to focus attention almost exclusively on heroic soldiers who fit the ideal 'all American profile'. And was there a better story to play up than a young, white female from the hills of West Virginia?

What about other soldiers who were killed or injured and held hostage during that ambush? Where is their national spotlight?

What about the stories of other military personnel? Thirty-five percent of U.S. military personnel are minorities, but you'd never know it by the media coverage, especially where heroism and sacrifice are concerned. How many media documentaries of black or Native American soldiers who were either killed or injured in the war have you seen on television?

Don't misunderstand me. I certainly don't mean to infer that our colorblind society doesn't always paint a balanced picture when it comes to American heroes. We just have our categories.

For example, black heroes are typically relegated to sports, music and entertainment. You won't find us on war related network news coverage, but you can always find us on MTV or ESPN!

And Native American heroes are relegated to wars in centuries past (but kept in the picture on the front of baseball caps and on the side of football helmets).

When it comes to serving this country in a war, saving people from a terrorist attack or a burning building, it's as if we don't exist. The media believes that Americans don't want to watch a documentary about a black person or Native American who did something of consequence that was truly heroic. They believe that stories like that won't make good copy.

However, given that the media is in the business of making money by selling newspapers, magazines, and television and radio advertising I can only assume that they promote what the public wants to see. Apparently stories about black and Native American war heroes won't generate much interest and revenue for them.

I want to recognize heroes who don't fit the 'all American' profile like Lori Piestewa and Shoshawna Johnson. Both women were members of the same unit as Jessica Lynch, and were ambushed in the same attack.

Lori Ann Piestewa

Pfc. Lori Ann Piestewa was a twenty-three year old Native American woman from Tuba City, Arizona. She was a member of the Hopi tribe, and a single mother with two young children.

Piestewa was the driver of the humvee that Jessica Lynch got into after Lynch's vehicle broke down near Nasiriyah. Under the direction of Master Sergeant Robert Dowdy, the four soldiers in the humvee took aggressive action to fight against the ambush. Unfortunately, a U.S. tractor trailer swerved around an Iraqi truck and jackknifed. As the humvee approached the truck it was hit on the driver's side by a grenade. Piestewa lost control of the humvee and hit the truck, killing Dowdy instantly.

Pfc. Piestewa was critically injured and taken to the same military hospital as Lynch. She died from severe head injuries shortly after her arrival.

Jessica Lynch gave Pfc. Piestewa direct credit for being instrumental in saving her life during the ambush. They were close friends and fellow soldiers in the same unit.

Lori Ann Piestewa was the first American woman and Native American to die in the war in Iraq. Her father and grandfather also served in the Army.

The Arizona government changed the name of a mountain in Phoenix, Arizona from Squaw Peak to Piestewa Peak in her honor. In addition, the Squaw Peak Freeway was changed to Piestewa Freeway.

Shoshawna Johnson

Army Specialist (Spc.) Shoshawna Johnson is a 30-year-old black woman from El Paso, Texas. She is a single parent with one daughter whose main job in the Army was to be a cook. Although she was principally trained to be a soldier, she was training to be a chef when she was deployed to the Middle East just before the war.

Spc. Johnson had both of her ankles shattered in the ambush. Following the ambush, she and four other Americans were held as prisoners of war (POW) by Iraqi soldiers. The Iraqis beat her when she was initially captured, and the beatings only stopped when the soldiers realized that she was a female. Johnson was separated from her male counterparts for a long period of time while being held hostage.

Videotape of the POW's being held was broadcast on Iraqi television. Johnson was shown sitting on a sofa looking very disorientated, eyes darting from side to side. One of her ankles was bandaged, and her arms were held close together in her lap. She was missing her boots.

Spc. Johnson and the other POW's were ultimately released on April 13, 2003, after twenty days in captivity.

Johnson was the first female American soldier to be captured during the war. Her father had also served in the Army, and was active in the 1991 Persian Gulf War.

155

RACE AND HYPOCRISY
...a few random thoughts

Chapter 17

A Kid From The Bronx

I am a product of a middle class family. My parents raised five children in a three-bedroom attached house in the Williamsbridge section of the Bronx. I am the oldest child, and my four younger siblings and I were born within an eleven-year time frame. We were all very close, and learned how to look out for each other, and share with one another as we were growing up.

My brothers Kyle, Kris and I shared the same bedroom. We had bunk beds and a pull-out bed for my youngest brother Kris. I remember being especially careful not to step on Kris when I was climbing down from the top bunk to go to the bathroom at night. My sisters, Robin and Raquel, also shared a small bedroom with a bunk bed.

Although our house was small in size, it was big in love and affection. This was entirely due to the love and discipline with which we were raised. We grew up in a Pentecostal church, and our upbringing was rooted in our family's religious faith and discipline. We were taught to respect ourselves and other people, and to this day we are all true to these principles.

My parents were both teachers in the New York City school system. My father, who passed away in May 1999, attended the City College of New York to study education. Prior to graduating from college, he was drafted by the Army and served in the Korean War. After being released from the military he went back to City College and completed both his Bachelor of Arts and Master of Arts degrees. Subsequently, he obtained a masters degree in guidance counseling from the City University of New York. He taught in the New York City school system for nearly thirty years before retiring in the early 1990's.

My mother graduated from Hunter College in New York with a degree in sociology and psychology. She worked for the New York City Department of Social Services as an investigator for several years, and then went back to Hunter College in the evening to earn the credits that were required to teach in the New York City school system. She became a substitute elementary school teacher and taught until my youngest sister, Raquel, who is the fourth child, was born. At that point, she stayed at home to be a full time homemaker. We benefited immensely from having our mother at home. She was always there for us and attentive to our needs as we were growing up. Our family was her principal focus.

I believe that my parents were terrific models of what children should have in their lives. In addition to growing up in a loving home, we were raised with discipline and structure, and the expectation that we would grow up to be responsible adults. In our house, family came first and education was the next priority. Our homework had to be completed before we could play or watch television. Our parents made sure that we studied, and they knew when we had exams and what our grades were. They also reviewed our report cards and attended parent/teacher conferences to make sure that we were doing the right things in school. We had more books than toys in our home. When I was in

157

junior high school, my father taught me how to fold the newspaper so that I could read it on the train.

Our parents demonstrated and preached personal responsibility, and accepted nothing less than us living up to our capabilities. Over the years, I have grown to respect them more and more for their parenting.

I only wish that all children were raised by responsible parents who are positive role models in their lives, and do not foster or accept excuses for failure. In my view, it all starts with parenting and clear expectations set for children. Children should grow up having fun and enjoying their lives, but they should also strive to do well academically and prepare themselves for the future.

We grew up on a street with a few dozen children our own respective ages. It was fun having extended families beyond the four walls of our house, and we could typically be found at a friend's house playing Uno, watching television, playing stick ball in the street on a nice day, or down at the playground immersed in one of our three-on-three basketball marathons. My friends and I lived on the basketball courts twelve months a year. During the winter we would even shovel the snow off the court, and play basketball with our gloves on.

The neighborhood was reasonably close-knit and well integrated when I was a kid. My elementary and junior high school experiences exposed me to kids from a wide variety of religious and ethnic backgrounds. Like most kids, I typically made friends with other kids whose personalities and interests were similar to mine. We all generally got along, and I can honestly say that I never felt out of place wherever I went in the neighborhood. I guess that at that time the Williamsbridge Section of the Bronx was about as diverse as any area of the city.

Although we are recognized as a black family, part of my ancestry is Native American.

My maternal grandmother's roots are both black and Native American. Her grandmother was the product of a marriage between a black slave and a full-blooded Cherokee Indian, who was born in the state of Virginia during slavery. At the age of thirteen or fourteen, my great grandmother was sold as a slave to a large family living in Abbeville, South Carolina.

When she arrived in South Carolina one of the rules was that she was not allowed to learn or even be taught to read. She lived with her owner's family, but did not understand what the place called 'school' was all about. However, every day she would play school games with the family's children, and in the process learned to read and write on her own. Her owner liked her quite a bit and decided after a period of time that she should be 'allowed' to get a formal education. She went on to become a teacher in South Carolina, and eventually married a black man. They had several children, among them my grandmother's mom.

We were educated by our parents about the legacy of our ancestor's struggles to simply learn how to read and write. Given this history, it was clear to each of us that in relative terms we didn't have it very hard. As long as we performed in school as expected we could have as much fun as we could handle within reasonable bounds.

Bronx High School of Science

I was a good student in junior high school, and it was my intention to go to Evander Childs High School in my neighborhood and play on the football team. However, my parents had other aspirations for me. They felt that I should attempt to be admitted into one of the New York City specialized high schools for students who were academically gifted. In order to get into one of these

159

schools I had to pass a competitive exam taken by many of the best students in the city.

I agreed to take the exam for the Bronx High School of Science, one of the specialized schools, in order to make my parents happy. I had absolutely no desire to go to Bronx Science. I knew that the odds of getting into that school were statistically no better than one in ten. But much to my surprise, and short-term chagrin, I made the cut and was admitted.

At Bronx Science my 'education' took on a new dimension, both socially and academically—*more socially than academically.* Up until that point in time, I had not had a lot of exposure to racial issues.

Starting high school was an eye opening experience for me. Many of my fellow classmates, most of whom were white, wondered out loud how *I* got into the school, even though I had to pass a standard city wide exam to get in. And some of my fellow students had all sorts of questions. "What score did you make to get in here?" I was repeatedly asked. I was also asked questions like "Are you here to play basketball? You speak real well – where are you from?"

I chose not to respond to their ignorant questions. There were no personal contacts involved, no family alumni ties, and no financial contributions that influenced my getting into the school. I got in by passing a competitive exam, the same exam that everyone else took.

And who ever heard of a basketball scholarship to a New York City public high school?

The difference, of course, was that many of my fellow students did not come from communities and environments that were as diverse as mine. They grew up believing that being among the best and brightest went hand-in-hand with being in a 'minority student free' environment.

At that time the population of black students at Bronx Science was probably around five percent at best. For the most part we stuck together in the interest of having a social network, and supporting each other through the academic and social challenges that we faced at the school. Our school cafeteria even had a section that was commonly known as the 'black table', and there was an unwritten rule that the black students sat there. It was our little 'hood.

Upon reflection, high school was very good for my personal development. I learned how to compete in a demanding academic environment, and how to deal with some of my peers who saw me as different - a minority who was 'lucky' to be among the best, but was expected to eventually sink in such a competitive environment.

I have to admit that I eventually came around to appreciating the opportunity to go to Bronx Science. At some point in my life I had to experience first hand the realities of life in America, where people can assume you are less capable, less intelligent, and less motivated because of your ethnicity.

It helped me learn that we cannot allow other people to define who we are and what we can achieve. Success starts with what our parents instill in us, and how we prepare ourselves for the future. That experience also prepared me for the next stop: Boston University.

Boston University

I started at Boston University in the mid 1970's, shortly after the conflict in Boston over the planned public school integration initiative. Busing students from economically disadvantaged neighborhoods to schools in better neighborhoods was viewed in part of the city as the best mechanism for improving the quality of education provided to *all* of the children in Boston, both academically and socially. The initiative was simply an attempt to level the educational playing field. Unfortunately, it created nothing more than significant conflict and racial tensions.

161

A simple alternative solution that some offered was to 'make all schools good and safe', whatever that means. I still hear that tired and unrealistic slogan where public education is concerned. Who was going to pay for the physical upgrades to the schools that needed them the most? Where was the money going to come from for new building systems like heating and air conditioning? How were the much needed furniture, supplies and textbooks and other learning materials going to be purchased? And who was going to teach in these schools?

To put it mildly, Boston was not the *friendliest* place for a minority student to begin his or her college education. However, Boston University had a good engineering program, and offered me a partial scholarship. In addition, there were several students from Bronx Science who I knew that went there.

There was also another significant reason that I went to college in Boston: my Aunt Kathy and Uncle Hubie Jones, and their eight children. While I was growing up, they used to visit us in the Bronx during the holidays, and I had the opportunity to spend time in their suburban Boston home on occasion. The family and I grew close through my childhood, and I knew that I would always be welcome in their home. They were my 'second' family, and I was treated like the eleventh member whenever I was there. To this very day I am close to them, and I appreciate all of the love and support that they have shown me over the years.

The student population in the university was about two or three percent black, and like my early days at Bronx Science I dealt with fellow students' curiosity about how I got admitted. From day one questions and comments from some of my freshman classmates, as well as other students living in my dormitory, pointed to the usual notions.

Surely I had to have fit the stereotype that was attached to a black kid at a very good private university: I had to have been an affirmative action student with marginal grades from a substandard high school in a poor neighborhood. For many students, and adults for that matter, it was inconceivable that my profile could have been any different. And even today that stereotype has not gone away. Although there are black and other minority students who are very good academically, and can perform successfully at the best colleges and universities, you wouldn't know it if you got all of your information from what you see on television or at the movies, or what you hear on the radio.

The reality was that my grades and SAT scores were probably better than most freshman students who started with me. I went to one of the best public high schools in the country, and I was fully qualified to be a student at the university. I was more than qualified with or without affirmative action. Ironically, it was often the students who weren't as academically prepared as I was who had the most questions about my 'qualifications'.

Don't misunderstand me.

Being an affirmative action student is *not* negative from my perspective. *I am strongly in favor of and have an appreciation for affirmative action programs.* I have benefited *immensely* from affirmative action. It has opened the door for students like me at schools that historically had no interest in having black students attend. As a result of the struggles of generations before me, I could apply and be admitted to a school like Boston University.

Being an affirmative action student does not mean that an individual is otherwise less capable than the other students. There are students from all types of backgrounds who are just as bright, hard working, motivated, and ambitious as their peers. However, through no fault of their own many of them do not have the benefits of being a student in a good quality school system. They may not have the same quality of resources available to them that others have to prepare for college.

For example, there are public school systems in this country today with social studies books that have Ronald Reagan as our 'current' President. Many schools are terribly understaffed, and students are forced to learn under extremely difficult circumstances. There are classrooms without adequate teaching materials, and with windows that do not fully close in the wintertime. Without question, the playing field is not even close to being level. As such, affirmative action gives students from different backgrounds an opportunity to compete at a variety of colleges and universities, taking into account the circumstances under which they got their pre-college educations.

Ironically, many non-minority students have been accepted into select colleges simply because of who they know or because of their family connections. Funny, but when *these* students are accepted for reasons other than *their* grades it no big deal!

They don't call it affirmative action; they call it 'connections'. Unfortunately, minority students typically do not have legacies of 'connections'. Many of us might actually be the first in our families to go to college. And this is not because our parents and grandparents never *wanted* the opportunity to get a good education themselves. The doors were too often simply closed, and thus they were systematically denied an education.

Fortunately, we are in a society where such disadvantages can be overcome.

The ability to get an education is there if a person really makes the effort to better themselves. Our parents and grandparents fought and died for the right to get an education, and we need to do everything that we can to take advantage of these opportunities regardless of the obstacles posed by society.

At some point in our lives we have to put our foot down, make a decision to be successful and go forward. And the situation may dictate that we do so with or without the support or approval of the world around us.

Basketball great Bill Russell once said, "I have never asked for equal opportunity and treatment. I demand it. As a citizen of this country it is my birthright. I accept nothing less than what I am simply due as an American citizen."

The Boston University experience turned out to be an interesting one. I always appreciated the students who were on the level with me, and who were clear about where I stood with them for better or for worse. Some wanted nothing to do with me, but most grew to get along with me just fine. We were on friendly terms regardless of where we were and what we were doing.

However, I did meet my share of the superficial types who predictably failed my 'see it live' test. I have become so good at sniffing out these types of folks that it has become easy for me.

We have all come in contact with the self-proclaimed 'ultra-liberal, color-blind, true friend to every American' types. These are the folks who supposedly have no hang-ups about race or religion, and will stand up to anyone who challenges the principles of equality for all men and women. They are proud to have you as a friend, and they love soul food, Motown music and the NBA. They also have friends just like you at home, etc., etc., etc.

I can usually spot them a mile away.

Typically, I would really get to see where the 'true friend to everyone' crowd stood when their parents and siblings were visiting. For example, I remember when one white female student's parents visited on Homecoming Day during my sophomore year. I met her when we were freshmen, and every time I was in her presence, regardless of the topic of conversation, she would somehow interject, "I relate really well to all types of people. My parents raised me that way. We go to a *very* mixed church. In high school my best friend was black..."

But for me seeing was and continues to be believing.

I made it a point to casually walk up to them while they were standing with her by the dormitory elevator. I am six feet three inches tall, and on that particular day I was wearing a maroon dashiki with a gold pattern, jeans and black leather sandals. At the time I had a seven-inch high afro and weighed about two hundred pounds.

Her father, who was no more than five and a half feet tall, turned around and looked up at me with an expression that would make you believe that a wall safe was about to fall on his head! His eyes were as wide as saucers.

So I introduced myself to her parents as their daughter's friend from the Bronx, New York. They just looked at me and said nothing. She looked at them, and then she looked at me and said nothing as well.

I offered a little information to lighten up the mood. Everyone gets warm and fuzzy when you know a little bit about him or her, so I said to her father, "I understand that you are an engineer. That's what I am studying. I might want to go to a good graduate engineering program like the one that you went to at Columbia. Maybe I could talk to you about it sometime. Your daughter and I talk all of the time, so I have come to learn a lot about your career."

Her poor dad got beet red. Obviously, his darling little 'friend to everyone' daughter had become comfortable enough with *me* to share details about their family.

We all got into the elevator, and went down to the lobby of the building. As they were leaving I grabbed and shook her father's hand, and then I put my arm around his daughter. I said to her, "Have fun. I'll see you Monday morning as usual." I hugged her, kissed her on the cheek, and took off in the other direction, laughing to myself all the way.

It remained to be seen what the test results would turn out to be. I came to suspect that her family's church wasn't as 'mixed' as I was led to believe, and that they had never met her 'black best friend' in high school. And as for 'standing up to anyone', something just didn't fit. My guess is that she probably didn't 'stand up' to her parents after our little social interaction.

And surprise, surprise! That was the very last conversation that I ever had with little miss "friend to everyone!' She could not stay far enough from me from that point until I graduated. And I can only imagine what the impact on her parents must have been like.

The ride home after the weekend must have been tense, with her father screaming and cursing all of the way down the highway, and her mother riding along with tears in her eyes biting on a clenched fist to keep from crying out loud.

I can also imagine her father having bad dreams about grandkids with little afros, and waking up in the middle of the night in a cold sweat - screaming. I can see him getting out of bed and walking around his yard in his pajamas and slippers, with a flashlight and a baseball bat looking for me.

I could go on about the number of students who failed the 'see it live' test while I was in college. Typical hypocrites. It was always interesting to see where people stood when their families were around.

But I'm comforted to know that such a scenario could not 'possibly' happen in today's wonderfully colorblind America. Wouldn't you agree?

None of my fellow Americans could be so hypocritical that they would even flinch in that situation today. Certainly not after 9/11, and all of the pronouncements that we are one big, happy, and united people.

~~ ·· ossibly be uncomfortable in that scenario now of anyone?

167

Chapter 18

Whose Country Is This Anyway?

The question of 'whose country this is' is one that fascinates me. So much of what is taught in our educational system, and is actually believed to be fact, is rooted in revisionist history.

In some ways I can understand why we have so many misconceptions about reality. Revisionist history has become the basis for how we see this country. And now we are struggling in our modern day society to deal with the reality of how this country is changing, and how these changes will totally reshape this culture. These changes scare a lot of traditionalists to death.

I can actually remember when I was in the third or fourth grade, and we were being taught a lesson about the so-called *discovery* of America. We are all probably familiar with the legend of Christopher Columbus, the great European hero who is credited with being responsible for the beginnings of our country. Columbus sailed over from Palos de la Frontera, Spain in the year 1492 with about ninety men and three ships: the Nina, the Pinta, and the Santa Maria.

During this lesson I raised my hand in front of my classmates and asked my teacher the following question:

168

"How did Columbus discover a new land when there were already people living here for many years? Weren't there Indians living here when he came over? How can you discover a place when people already live there?"

Even a grade school child could see through the *stupid* idea that a place could be 'discovered' *after* other people had been living there for thousands of years. If the Indians were here first *they* would have discovered this land. Or was I confused?

My teacher was a woman who looked very much like Aunt Bea from the Andy Griffith Show, only not quite as attractive. Her typical attire was a flower patterned dress that would give you a headache, with her hair tied up on top of her head by a big ribbon. Admittedly, I wasn't much better. I still have pictures of me in the third grade in my 'high water' pants, carrying my vinyl book bag and a metal superheroes lunch box.

She stammered some incoherent answer about Columbus starting colonies, and then she attempted to continue the stroll through the historical fantasyland. We were only eight or nine year old children, so the expectation was probably that we would buy anything. But I just didn't get it, so I raised my hand again.

"Weren't the Indians living here for lots of years before Columbus came over?"

This time she got angry and responded, "The history book says that Columbus discovered America. Not Indians. So please don't interrupt me again."

The woman was a certified educator, and the best answer that she could think of was, "because the history book says so". So we went on to learn about the settlers and the meetings with the Indians to share the land, and the first Thanksgiving, etc., etc.

I will never forget that day.

In my mind, I can picture some guy dressed like a fugitive from a Captain Crunch cereal box floating down the Hudson River in his fiberglass rowboat. He pulls up to the cruise ship terminal along the west side of Manhattan, and jumps out and begins to stroll across 42nd Street telling passersby that he just discovered Manhattan.

At some point in the day he is stopped by the police and taken to the psychiatric ward at Bellevue Hospital to be evaluated and is ultimately committed. And his story becomes the joke of the day on the local news.

Even in a city like New York, which has no shortage of imaginative folks walking the streets on the average day, he would be flagged as a nut.

I have sometimes thought that maybe I should take a cruise to the Cayman Islands on the famous cruise liner 'Moe, Larry, and Curly', and plant a flag in the port and declare that I have discovered a new land!! Makes sense to me. And it should make sense to all of those who believe American history as it has been taught to us. Certainly the logic is consistent.

That's how absurd the 'Columbus discovered America' folk tale is. It's a shame that almost forty years after I was in elementary school the same nonsense is being taught in our education system, and the next generation of children will grow up believing that you can discover a place where people had *already* lived for thousands of years.

And this little history lesson was also taught to me at a time in my life when I was supposed to learn the song, 'My country 'tis of thee, sweet land of liberty…land where my fathers died, land of the pilgrims pride…'

But when I think about it I guess that in a sense the song is accurate.

My fathers died… on slave ships and plantations, and the pilgrims pride…was rooted in the destruction of Native American culture in the name of expansionism.

Honestly, would anybody in his or her right mind expect a black or Native American student to want to sing this song? There are many people like me who are descendants of *both* bloodlines.

So of course, being the inquisitive, non-conformist child that I was, I asked the same teacher what the song meant to people who were 'Indians or from a slave history' since I was a descendant of both. And once again the best answer that she could give me was, "It's in the social studies book, and all boys and girls should learn it."

Why don't we call history what it is?

Simply put, when Columbus arrived, the destruction of Native American life as it existed began to take place. Consequently, the blueprint for destroying much of the Native American culture was firmly in place when the pilgrims landed on Plymouth Rock in the year 1620. The expressed intent of the settlers was simply to establish colonies for European migration into the territory, and if the Native Indians were in the way they were either killed or enslaved.

Another fact is that the settlers didn't come here because they were courageous and adventurous explorers who took on the challenges of sailing to a new land while facing danger. They came here because they were being persecuted in their own land.

Throughout the following few hundred years the systematic expansion of America by the settlers and their descendants went hand in hand with the continued destruction and abuse of Native American peoples.

And along the path of expansionism Africans were enslaved to build this country.

Did I misstate something?

The revisionist version of American history would have you believe that the Native Americans and European settlers began their relationship by shaking hands, throwing a picnic and playing a friendly coed softball game, and then going out building harmonious communities. It's simply denial at its best!

Yet we allow our children to believe the arrogant notion that civilization didn't begin *until* the settlers showed up. For anyone with a drop of Native American blood in them, or an ounce of common sense for that matter, the entire notion is both ludicrous and insulting. The implications are that Native Americans were some beings that just existed and were not validated as people until the settlers arrived.

I still live in the state of Connecticut, which is home to a number of Native American tribes, all of whose roots were well established *before* the settlers arrived. For example, the Pequot tribe, which went on to build the Foxwoods Casino, was among the original inhabitants of the New England region. They are among the 'aboriginals or indigenous people' – translation: native to a particular place or living in a natural area. The Pequots numbered approximately eight thousand individuals, inhabiting two hundred and fifty square miles of land in the early 1600's. Before the settlers arrived the only concerns that the tribe faced was protecting *their* territory from potential intrusion from other tribes.

In the year 1614 a Dutch explorer by the name of Adriaen Block sailed up the Long Island Sound and on to the Connecticut River to what is now the City of Hartford. Like Columbus and his so-called 'discovery', Mr. Block was credited with discovering Connecticut. Subsequently, in the year 1620, European settlers arrived and over the next several years established their footing by developing fur and wampum trading relationships with the Pequots.

In the year 1632, the settlers began to negotiate with the Pequots to build a fort and trading post on land hunted by the tribe. This relationship lasted until the year 1636, when the settlers burned down a Pequot Village and killed a tribal leader in retaliation for an attack on European traders who began trading on land historically occupied by the tribe.

It simply wasn't enough for the settlers to arrive, and set up in their new world and come to some understanding about what would be their space. Expansionism was the objective, so they attempted to move into land clearly inhabited by the tribe. This conflict increased the level of hostility between factions, which led to the Pequot War.

Within a year, the colonies that had been established in Connecticut and Massachusetts prepared for war against the Pequots. Together with two tribes in the area, they attacked the Pequots in the spring of 1637 and killed thousands, leaving the tribe with about six hundred remaining members.

When the war ended in the fall of 1638, the surviving Pequots were either divided up among the other tribes or sold into slavery. It wasn't until 1666 that they were able to establish a reservation on about 3,000 acres of land that was returned to them by the government of Connecticut.

Over the next several decades, they fought in several wars in an attempt to survive. By the mid 1800's, the tribe's land had been reduced to two hundred acres, and in the early 1900's the total Pequot population was only 42 members.

It was not until the 1970's that tribal members began to move back to the reservation and embark on a series of economic initiatives, including taking legal action to recover land stolen from them over the course of history. In 1983, the federal government granted the Pequots tribal recognition, and allowed the tribe to repurchase stolen land in the state of Connecticut. Through their incredible will to survive and their fight to re-establish themselves, and go

173

forward in a hostile environment, they were able to build the Foxwoods Resort Casino.

This is just one of hundreds of examples of the fight by Native Americans to survive in this country. Yet American history romanticizes the relationship between the Native Americans and Europeans as neighborly until the *Indians* became the problem! Talk about a twisting reality. The Native Americans were doing just fine before they were invaded by the settlers.

Ironically, the term that we use today to describe a group of people that would go to a place that they are not native to, establish residence, and then attempt to destroy its inhabitants through the murder of its people and the destruction of their homes is *terrorists*.

Let's compare scenarios. The settlers went to a place that they were not native to, established residence, and then attempted to destroy its inhabitants through the murder of its people and the destruction of their homes. By our own American standards they were *terrorists*. The only difference in this scenario is that if you accept the sanitized version of American history when the settlers killed innocent people in their native land their actions were perfectly fine.

How can it be that we can abhor and fight terrorism, and celebrate it at precisely the same time?

Once again, it's about the 'who' as opposed to the 'what' of the issue.

Come on, you say. I'm just playing word games. *Colonists, terrorists, colonists, terrorists, we know that they couldn't possibly mean the same thing.* Besides, why is this even relevant?

I have often heard, "all of what happened is in the past and folks are tired of hearing about it. Why do people even bring it up? Get over it." But the reality is that this country makes light of its 'proud' history continually.

174

For example, wouldn't you think that the annual celebration of Columbus Day makes light of the Native American experience? Yet we chose to celebrate a day that is in recognition of an individual who planted the seeds for the destruction of Native Americans.

What about Thanksgiving? Kids dressing up like pilgrims and Native Americans aren't consistent reminders? When history is brought up it's viewed as *'simply in the past.'* However, when these holidays come around they are called *celebrations*.

The reality is that as long as certain holidays are on the calendar, and children are taught revisionist history in our schools the so-called past will always be alive and relevant.

And how about the old cowboys and Indians movies that you can still watch on television? The movies where the American heroes fight the dreaded, savage, ignorant Indians whose sole purpose in life is to do harm to the honorable and friendly settlers?

What about the degrading sports mascots, specifically symbols like the Atlanta Braves mascot and their war paint and tomahawk chop, the Cleveland Indians' red-faced mascot, and the Washington Redskins logo on their helmets?

As an aside, I can't help but comment on the football game played every season in Dallas between the Cowboys and the Washington Redskins. At these games, two middle-aged African American 'gentlemen' have traditionally dressed up as a cowboy and a Native American and chased each other around for the national television cameras. They fail to realize that while they carry on mocking Native Americans with the dancing, tomahawk-swinging stereotype, the world sees two ignorant black men doing what amounts to a modern-day *Step 'n' Fetchit* routine.

Without question, ignorance comes in *all* colors.

175

But I know what you're thinking. The effects of the European invasion, and the theft of Native American land, really doesn't have as many on-going reminders as I believe there are. I am simply paranoid. Maybe I should take a nice drive this weekend to clear my paranoid mind.

Let's see. I know. I live in *New England*. Maybe I'll take a drive through Connecticut. I can visit New Britain, New London, Bristol, East Lyme, Manchester, Norwich, Oxford, Chester, Colchester, Derby, Durham, Glastonbury, Plymouth, Preston, Salisbury, Stamford, Stratford, Windsor, or Woodstock.

Or maybe I'll drive up to Massachusetts. I can stop in places like Cambridge, New Bedford, Dorchester, Plymouth, Barnstable, Bellingham, Beverley, Boston, Bridgewater, Brighton, Leicester, Lincoln, Marlborough, Northampton, Oxford, Chatham, Dedham, Dover, Falmouth, Gloucester, Yarmouth, Salisbury, Reading, Sheffield, Shrewsbury, Sudbury, Taunton, Tewksbury, Wareham, Hull, Ipswich, Weymouth, Winchester, Worcester, or Yarmouth.

All cities or towns right here that are named after cities or towns in England.

On second thought, I think that I'll stay home. The *New England* Patriots are playing the Washington *Redskins*.

Seriously, to this day the average American can't seem to grasp how Native Americans and black folks can have a problem with traditional American history as it is taught. *There is absolutely no sensitivity or recognition of how insulting it is to expect us to share the enthusiasm for American history that white America does.*

I know that to expect American history to be taught differently than how it is perpetuated in our education system is a pipe dream. It will never happen. If I had asked my teachers in elementary school why history couldn't be taught more realistically, they probably would have told me that it would have been too expensive to print all new history books. I'm sure that I would have been given answers just as brilliant as the ones that I got about Christopher Columbus and 'My Country 'Tis of Thee'.

However, I do believe that those of us who know better have a *responsibility* to teach history as it really happened to our youth. Black and Native American children in particular should not be allowed to grow up with the notion that we are second-class citizens in this country because history books and fourth-grade teachers tell them about all the wonderful things that made America what it is. By and large, our children are still educated with the intentional exclusion of the straightforward facts about our history.

They should learn about the struggles their ancestors experienced just to survive, and the battles that have been fought for all of us to have the rights and freedoms that we can easily take for granted.

They should learn about the many contributions that our ancestors have made to this country's development. And they should learn the names and stories of Native American and black educators, inventors, entrepreneurs, artists, freedom fighters, etc.

Unfortunately, too many of our children are simply allowed to learn only what is in the 'history book'. In my opinion, this is a contributing factor to why many of our youth have a negative self-image.

The responsibility for educating children starts with the *parents*, and should not be simply deferred to the school system. Without question, the more knowledgeable children are, the more prepared they will be to deal with the challenges of living in America. They will be less likely to accept the attitudes that they will encounter as they grow up in this 'color blind' society, and more likely to put their feet down and demand equal status without hesitation.

If you want a real view of American history, visit a Native American reservation or museum sometime. By the end of the day, the confusion about 'who' discovered 'what' should end. When you are finished, pay a visit to a Museum of African American History and see who the original 'employees' were who built this country. You just might clear up even more of your confusion.

Chapter 19

Happy Holidays?

From some people's perspectives, the existence of several national holidays does not exactly call for a celebration either. Like the Native American population, some holidays are no more than annual reminders of American history.

Let me start with *New Year's Day*. This one is easy – who could argue with starting a new year? The prospect of out with the old and in with the new. A new start in a new year.

Martin Luther King's Birthday. I'll address this one last.

President's Day. This particular holiday honors Presidents George Washington and Abraham Lincoln, two individuals with a jaded history specific to slavery and race relations.

179

George Washington became a slave owner in the year 1743, when he was eleven years old. He had inherited his slave labor upon the death of his father. As he entered his twenties, he used his slaves to farm the land on his estate in Mount Vernon, Virginia. When he reached the age of twenty-seven he married Martha, who was also a slave owner. They combined their 'resources' to live comfortably on the backs of the servants and laborers who did all of the work. At the time of his death in the year 1799, George and Martha Washington owned three hundred and sixteen slaves on their Mount Vernon estate.

OK, so Mr. Washington wasn't such an honorable man, but how about Abraham Lincoln?

Mr. Lincoln has been cast as the true friend of black America, and the man who freed the slaves - a true hero. However, he is the same man who made a speech in front of a black audience stating that, "It is better for the Negro and white races to be separated. You and we are different races. We have between us a broader physical difference than exists between any other two races. Your race suffers very greatly, many of them, by living among us, while ours suffers from your presence. In a word, we suffer on each side. If this be admitted, it affords a reason, at last, why we should be separated. Even when you cease to be slaves, you are yet far removed from being placed on equality with white people. *On this broad continent not a single man of your race is made the equal of a single man of ours.*"

Not all slaves were freed by Mr. Lincoln, only those slaves from states that chose to end their efforts to continue the practice of slavery for political reasons. It was in Lincoln's *political best interest* not to have to deal with the states that were home to a rising population of 'contentious' slaves who were challenging the system.

Not quite my definition of a hero.

And another highly-revered President who merits discussion, although he doesn't have a holiday in his honor, is Thomas Jefferson.

Mr. Jefferson was also a slave owner. According to his own records, at the age of thirty-one, he inherited slaves from his mother and father-in-law on his property in Monticello, Virginia. After the death of his wife in the year 1782, he maintained his 'slave inventory' for another forty-four years until his death at eight-three years old.

Along the way, Mr. Jefferson found it desirable to have sexual relations with at least one of his slaves, a woman named Sally Hemings.

Miss Hemings was thirty years younger than Mr. Jefferson. He inherited her as a child, and at the age of fourteen she accompanied Mr. Jefferson's daughter to France in the capacity of being her nurse. When Miss Hemings returned to Monticello at the age of sixteen, she continued working in Mr. Jefferson's home as a maid. He treated her as a 'special slave' and a relationship developed.

Miss Hemings gave birth to five children while living at Monticello, and at least one of the children was fathered by Mr. Jefferson. Her five children, who were eventually freed by Mr. Jefferson, were some of the very few slaves that he ever afforded that opportunity.

Mr. Jefferson is the same great American hero who happens to be the author of the Declaration of Independence written in 1776. According to this document, "...all men are created equal, that they are endowed by their creator with certain unalienable rights, that among them are life, liberty, and the pursuit of happiness."

All of this done while he owned an inventory of slaves.

He also said in a letter that he wrote in 1814 that, "the amalgamation of whites with blacks produces a degradation which no lover of his country...can innocently consent." I guess that fathering at least one (known) black child was just an innocent *indiscretion* on his part, and his

181

contribution to the supposed degradation of this country was just a little mistake.

As usual, I'm confused.

On the one hand, this country is the home of separatists who have major issues regarding (among other things) interracial relations, and at the same time these people can hold a man like Thomas Jefferson in high esteem.

I would think that his name would be held in infamy. But what do I know.

Columbus Day and *Thanksgiving* have already been addressed.

Memorial Day is another reminder of how blacks fought and died in wars, and how those who survived came home to a country without having any rights and were treated like they were the enemy.

Where *Independence Day, Labor Day* and *Christmas* are concerned there is not much to comment about.

Which leaves *Martin Luther King Day.*

Born in 1929 in Atlanta, Georgia, Martin Luther King, Jr. became an ordained minister in 1947, and in 1954 became the pastor of a church in Montgomery, Alabama. During the following year he led a boycott of the segregated bus lines in the city after Rosa Parks was arrested for refusing to sit in the back of the bus simply because she was black. This boycott led to the desegregation of city bus lines in 1956, after the Supreme Court ruled that bus segregation was illegal.

In 1956, King formed the Southern Christian Leadership Conference to continue the fight for civil rights and an end to racial discrimination. In 1963 he led a successful campaign to desegregate public entities in Birmingham. He also led the historic March on Washington that was attended by an estimated two hundred and fifty thousand people. As a result of his efforts, he was awarded a Nobel Peace Prize in 1964, and was instrumental in the passage of the Civil Rights Bill signed into law that year.

In 1965, Dr. King also led a demonstration in Selma, Alabama to protest discriminatory practices in the voting process. This demonstration ultimately played a role in the passage of the Voting Rights Act later that year.

The following year Dr. King established the Poor People's Campaign, which was focused on jobs and equal treatment for *all* poor people. The campaign had planned a March on Washington in 1968 to protest for employment opportunities and an end of housing discrimination against the poor. However, the plan was interrupted by Dr. King's participation in a march supporting striking sanitation workers in Memphis, Tennessee. On April 4, 1968 Dr. King was assassinated while standing on the balcony of the Lorraine Motel in Memphis.

During his lifetime, Dr. King was a significant figure in the movement to end segregation and improve the lives of minorities and poor people of *all* backgrounds. He organized movements to address the effects of unemployment, job and housing discrimination, and the need for legislation aimed at ensuring equal treatment for all Americans under the law.

In 1968, just *days* after Dr. King's assassination, Congressman John Conyers introduced legislation for the institution of a federal holiday in King's honor. After being rejected in the beginning, the proposal was resubmitted during each ensuing legislative session, and after tremendous pressure in 1982 and 1983 Congress finally passed the legislation. Subsequently, President Reagan signed the legislation into law in 1983. However, although the legislation passed in 1983 it was not until 1999 that all fifty states formally instituted the holiday.

In spite of the tremendous contribution that Dr. King made to achieve equality for all Americans, *his* holiday still leaves a bitter taste in the mouths of many people. For some, national holidays and monuments for terrorists, slave owners, and segregationists are perfectly reasonable and acceptable, but holidays for civil rights activists who fight for all people are not. How's that for logic?

The greatest example of disrespect for Dr. King's legacy —and for black people and other minorities in general— comes from none other than George Bush. Bush believes that the King holiday has represented the perfect opportunity to attempt to set back the gains made by blacks and other minorities, and to appoint a racist judge to the federal appeals court.

On Dr. King's birthday in 2003, Bush announced his decision to ask the U.S. Supreme Court to overturn the University of Michigan's affirmative action program stemming from a reverse discrimination case filed against the university. For most of America the effort to perpetuate the myth that affirmative action is unnecessary because we are a 'color-blind' society continues on. Fortunately, the normally conservative Supreme Court saw through Bush's attempt to pander to the institutional denial of many Americans regarding the status of equal opportunity in this country, and did not force the university to abandon its affirmative action program. But Bush wasn't quite finished, and found another way to kick black people in the teeth again on the King Holiday in 2004.

This time he was determined to appoint Charles Pickering, a District Court Judge from Mississippi, to a seat on the 5th U.S. Court of Appeals in New Orleans, Louisiana. This court handles appeals in the states of Mississippi, Texas and Louisiana. The Democrats had blocked Pickering's nomination for more than two years, largely because he had an anti-civil rights and anti-woman's rights history.

So what did Bush do? He waited until Congress was in recess and bypassed it by installing Mr. Pickering through a procedure known as a recess appointment, which does not require a confirmation by the legislature. Ironically, this appointment was made just one day after he laid a wreath on Dr. King's grave.

Among Judge Pickering's 'achievements' was his 1994 reduction of the sentence of a man convicted of burning a cross on the lawn of an interracial couple living in Mississippi, and firing gunshots into their home. The assailant and two of his friends built an eight foot cross, put it up on the couple's lawn, and doused it with gasoline and set it on fire.

Because the case involved a cross burning, it was initially handled by the federal Justice Department's Office of Civil Rights, which allowed two of the assailants to plea-bargain down to misdemeanor crimes with no jail time. The pleas were accepted in one case because the assailant had a low IQ (obviously not too low to figure out how to build and burn a cross), and because other the assailant was seventeen years old (obviously not too young to build and burn a cross).

Judge Pickering went against the Civil Rights Division's recommendation of a seven and a half year jail term for the third assailant, even though he was found guilty of the crime with no plea bargain involved. He felt that the sentencing recommendation was too harsh relative to the others, and he ultimately asked the Civil Rights Division to tell him what the sentencing standards were in other federal courts. The Civil Rights Division decided to let Judge Pickering determine the term of the sentence, and he settled for a whopping twenty-seven months! I guess that the significance of cross-burnings in his mind was *over rated!*

However you cut it, this appointment of such a racially insensitive justice was a clear and strong slap in the face of black people by George Bush.

So am I seeing this holiday picture the wrong way? I know, it's all past history, and what does all of this history have to do with today? Why do I bring it up?

Because the last time I checked, all of these holidays were still on my calendar!

Because the last time that I went shopping, three segregationist American heroes were on the one-dollar bill, five-dollar bill, penny, nickel, and quarter.

Because the last time that I visited Washington D.C. I couldn't help coming face to face with the Washington, Jefferson, and Lincoln Monuments (I guess slavery had its rewards).

My point is that this country continues the tradition of honoring racists and slave owners instrumental in destroying black and Native American culture, and the reminders are everywhere.

I for one see several of our national holidays as continuing examples of how distorted the average American's view of history is. Sad but true.

Chapter 20

Capitalism – The American Way! So What's The Problem?

Much of the public and political structure in this country takes issue with how much revenue casinos on Native American reservations generate, their non-tax status (which is typically at the state level), and the total control that the respective tribes exercise over their businesses.

For example, Connecticut is home to two very profitable casinos, Foxwoods Resort, which is on the Mashantucket reservation, and the Mohegan Sun on the Mohegan reservation. Each casino operation is governed by a tribal council that selects the management team that runs all aspects of the day-to-day operation. The casinos have created thousands of employment opportunities, and brought a significant amount of tourism to the area. Clearly they have been economically successful, and brought fun and excitement to the millions of visitors who frequent them annually. We call this type of business in the corporate world a thriving economic engine.

The casinos are located on the tribe's ancestral land, much of which they were able to recover after years of resistance. The federal Indian Reorganization Act of 1934 recognized Native American tribes, and gave them the right to purchase land adjacent to their reservations, and to incorporate the newly acquired property into their reservation under a tax-free status at the state level.

In 1983, the Pequot Indian Tribe was formally recognized by the federal government. In 1989, the Pequots formally requested to begin negotiations to build a casino on their Mashantucket reservation. William O'Neill, the Governor of Connecticut, and other elected officials met this request with strong resistance. This resistance was partly due to the fact that under the Indian Gaming Regulatory Act of 1988 (IGRA) casinos on federally recognized reservations could not be subject to taxation.

You can imagine how thrilled the residents of the affected towns were. Prime tax-free land was to be used for a money making proposition. How unfair!

The IGRA mandated that the state begin negotiations with the Pequots, but Governor O'Neill ignored the requirement. After being ignored, the Pequots had to appeal to a federal district court to order the state to grant them a casino license. The judge ordered the Governor to comply with the requirement to negotiate with the Pequots.

But instead of treating the Pequots with the proper respect, Governor O'Neill appealed to the U.S. District Court system and lost his appeal. This development eventually forced the issue to the Supreme Court. Finally, in 1991, the Supreme Court ruled in favor of the Pequots and Foxwoods was on the road to being built.

I would think that in this land of truth, justice, and the American way, the residents of Connecticut would have been *thrilled* to see Native Americans recover what was stolen from them and build a successful business enterprise, especially since they would live in their own separate community. We have many communities in Connecticut where Native Americans and other minorities are practically invisible, which seems to make a lot of people quite pleased. So what was the problem with this development?

And what would the average American do if their property were taken from them or the family – walk away? No. There would be lawsuits, violence, anything to get their property back. And as for the sovereignty issue, when the average American experiences a wrong and goes through legal channels and wins their case are they simply done? Of course not. They want a big monetary settlement, punitive damages for pain and suffering! In this case, the Native Americans wanted a tax-free status for their pain and suffering.

So what was the issue? Once again, it's not about the 'what' it's about the 'who'.

A more recent example of what I am talking about was covered in a January 2004 Hartford Courant newspaper article regarding the formal recognition of the Connecticut-based Schaghicoke Tribal Nation by the federal government. Rather than describe the article I will give you the actual highlights and my commentary in *italics*.

Just a word of warning. Be careful. The hypocrisy may be damaging to your eyes.

Title: A Nation Once Again

"The federal Bureau of Indian Affairs (BIA) overturned a previous decision and recognized a fourth state Indian tribe, the Kent-based Schaghticoke Tribal Nation – making more casinos an increasingly likely possibility in Connecticut and sparking a new firestorm over tribal gaming here."

Why was there a firestorm? If General Motors wanted to open a new plant in Connecticut the population would be thrilled. Aren't we all for economic development and the creation of jobs? Wouldn't a growth in tourism bring welcome revenues to any state?

"In 2002, the BIA recognized the North Stonington-based Eastern Pequots, again combining two rival groups. Both the Eastern Pequots and the Schaghticokes are backed by wealthy investors who want to bankroll gambling casinos..."

There's nothing like a shot at making a lot of money that makes those 'dreaded' Indians such attractive

189

business partners. Even John Wayne would want a partnership.

"Thursday's decision stunned state and local officials who have fought the federal recognition, dramatizing a cultural and communications gap between 21st century Indian tribes and local and state government."

Hold on. You mean to tell me that there are still cultural and communications gaps between Native Americans and the rest of society? What a revelation. Yet I seem to recall that we are all one people (see a recent speech from any politician running for national office). Why is this gap suddenly so relevant?

"This approach (the overturn of a recent decision which now favors the tribe) means that the evidence no longer counts for anything. The precedent is so astonishing...that it should awaken Congress to the BIA's arbitrary and law-less approach" said Attorney General Richard Blumenthal.

I suppose that the tribe should feel guilty. After all, the government has always treated them and their ancestors in a totally 'lawful' manner. Decisions have never been made arbitrarily regarding the treatment of their people.

"It had to be politics," said Blumenthal, "Many of these tribal groups have friends in positions of power. They have succeeded in using that power behind the scenes."

Is he serious? Since colonization, the government of this country has been run by descendents of the settlers, and Native Americans had little to no power, and in many cases, barely survived. Now Native Americans have begun to establish political power in some areas of the country, and can play the same game as the power brokers and use political influence to get what they want.

Are they doing things in a way that makes them different than the other participants in the political structure as it exists otherwise? Are they somehow different?

Absolutely. It's perfectly fine for the Presidents, Governors, Mayors, Senators, Congressmen and

190

Congresswomen, lobbyists and even Attorney Generals to successfully play the political power game. But Native Americans? Now that's stepping over the line! How dare they use power behind the scenes!

"We celebrate this long-awaited decision regarding the Schaghticokes...said Eastern Pequot Chairman Marcia Jones Flowers...Despite the struggles still ahead, the Schaghticokes now have the opportunity to provide for their members' health, education, and housing needs, which are so critical to us all."

Imagine that. The ability to be self-sufficient and take care of their own needs. Maybe our government can learn a lesson because there are too many people who cannot afford health care, our education infrastructure is crumbling, and we have an epidemic of homelessness and people living in sub-standard housing.

"The Schaghticoke Tribal Nation decision is Exhibit One that the federal government is presiding over a corrupt process that disregards the will of the communities and states most adversely impacted by these decisions...Jeff Benedict, president of the Connecticut Alliance Against Casino Expansion said."

Did he say corruption with regard to Native American rights to their native land and the pursuit of capitalism?

And as far as a disregard for the will of the affected communities, don't we continue to openly celebrate the 'accomplishments' of certain historical figures because they had no regard for existing communities? They simply did what they wanted without a concern for those individuals who were 'most adversely impacted'. Apparently it was fine when it was called expansionism.

I wonder if Mr. Benedict celebrates Thanksgiving?

I'd love to see another casino in Connecticut. I'd love to see a new casino every five miles. It is about time that a piece of history begins to right itself. Native Americans just want to participate in the American dream and practice

191

capitalism—and they're not even looking to use slave labor to do it. So what's the problem?

Unfortunately, there is no end in site to the battle against opposition to what is rightfully being pursued by Native Americans. For example, there has been a movement in the State of New York to tax the sale of petroleum and tobacco products sold by the Seneca Nation of Indians on their reservations. Such a change in the laws would be a clear violation of past treaties, among them the Buffalo Creek Treaty of 1842 that makes the Seneca Nation a sovereign nation that is excluded from this type of taxation.

The Seneca Nation pays federal income taxes, and its members are only exempt from New York state taxes if they both live and work on reservations. They do not add a state sales tax to their goods, and therefore do not pass on such a sales tax to the government. If such a tax was implemented, it is estimated that hundreds of Native American and non-Native American employees would lose their employment because of anticipated lost sales.

Historically, the initiative to tax the sale of these products has been pushed by the National Association of Convenience Stores (NYACS), which has a large part of the sales base in the state. They have lobbied state legislators to impose an illegal tax in order to hurt the tribe's ability to compete in the market.

In 2003, after several years of continued protests from the NYACS, New York State passed legislation to tax these products beginning in May 2004. The Seneca Nation fought the legislation, and in February 2004 the state government decided to postpone the implementation of taxes on the products sold on the reservations. This 'postponement' was met with protests from the NYACS which sees the ruling as unfair. Even in the year 2004, treaties cannot simply be honored without being challenged. The assault on Native Americans continues...

Chapter 21

I'd Like A Snoop Dogg CD and an Allen Iverson Jersey Please!

It has to be difficult to be a kid from the comfortable suburbs of Anytown, USA. Imagine having to hide in your room while you listen to rap music through your headphones. The fact is that the largest consumers of rap and hip-hop music CD's and videos in this country are white kids, so there must be a lot of anxiety out there. But there is always an out for them – they can tell their parents that they are listening to someone like Barry Manilow if they get questioned.

And as for the football and basketball jerseys? Wearing a jacket over them will work just fine until the kids are out of the house and on their way to the movies, school, or the mall. Then they can lose the jacket, and show the jersey and crank the music! And as for teenage fashion? Clothing lines like FUBU and others are worn by kids from all types of backgrounds.

But if I were them I wouldn't worry too much. A generation ago *their* parents had to hide in their closets as they enjoyed black culture under the cover of darkness.

Singing groups like the Temptations, Supremes, O'Jays, Chi-Lites, Stylistics, Manhattans, Smokey Robinson and the Miracles, and Harold Melvin and the Blue Notes (the list can go on forever) sold billions of albums in the white community.

Athletes like Hank Aaron, Willie Mays, Bob Gibson, Julius Erving, Kareem Abdul Jabbar, Jim Brown, and Mean Joe Greene entertained millions of their parents who sat in front of their television sets for hours at a time.

Many of their parents even enjoyed a good meal from the darkest corner of a soul food restaurant.

Yet there are *still* folks who would dread the day that I buy the house next door. And these same folks will listen to and purchase black music, wear black athlete's jerseys and eat traditionally black food. They will even pay steep prices to go to a sporting event or an R&B music concert.

So what's the catch? I must admit that I'd normally be confused, but I *think* that I have this one figured out.

For these 'open minded types' all of these activities require just about *zero* interaction with black folks! They can purchase and listen to black music without the threat of one of us coming into their personal space. They can go to a sporting event with ticket prices too expensive for the average black person, and be entertained by their favorite black athletes without the fear of sitting next to one of us.

And have you ever been to an R&B concert? They are typically as integrated a public activity as you will ever see in this country. Everybody's dancing and singing, and having a great time. But then again concerts are not exactly social events that require any real interaction amongst folks. Besides, the lights are out so there is little risk of being seen among 'those' people.

They can go to a soul food restaurant and huddle up at a table close to the door just in case a riot or police raid breaks out. Okay, this option requires *some* level of interaction. But it's black folks waiting on tables, preparing the meals, and cleaning up after everyone is finished eating, which for some Americans is the natural order of the universe anyway.

And when the evening is over they can go back to the security and comfort of their homes knowing that the police will pull someone like me over if I should dare to drive down their street.

I call it integration by convenience. When it comes to being entertained or fed from a distance 'integration' works out just fine. For many Americans black culture is both interesting and enjoyable until a direct interaction with us on equal terms with no hang-ups or prejudices is necessary. Then the lines are drawn, and it's time to be reminded that this 'all men are created equal' stuff is *over rated.*

For example, for some folks it's bad enough to have to work with us. And it's especially embarrassing to have to admit to a family member that they work *for* one of us if they should happen to. I have personally experienced that phenomenon on several occasions.

I've had subordinates avoid me at Christmas parties or other social gatherings because they did not want to introduce their spouses to me. Maybe they would have been viewed as less than a man (it was almost always a male) when they got home. I've also had employees keep their kids from me at the company picnic. Gee, I wonder why.

Conversely, one of the most glaring examples of the hypocrisy in this country is the relationship between black professional athletes and performers, and their business agents who are usually white attorneys.

When millions of dollars are involved, the black person becomes the boss, a good friend, golfing buddy, and someone to introduce to their family, friends and colleagues. These agents cannot get into the athletes and performers' wallets fast enough. In plain English, they are a meal ticket.

If these folks couldn't catch a football or sing a note they wouldn't get the time of day. They would be another suspect to be feared while walking down the street. Or maybe just another black guy in a business suit on the train to or from Connecticut. I get the feeling that if I were a highly paid athlete or performer sitting *alone* on the train would be virtually impossible to do.

I would have my friendly fellow Connecticut attorneys climbing over each other to sit next to me, wanting to discuss business opportunities or get a shot at representing me. Investment banker types would want to have lunch with me or look to set up a golf date with an interest in managing my financial portfolio. And I would certainly get invited to charity fundraisers.

Women would want me to sign autographs for their husbands, boyfriends, children, parents, brothers, sisters, and pets – and maybe sit next to me (as long as my hands are in full view). But if I decided that I wanted to sit alone and read my newspaper they would be insulted. I'm sure that money and fame would make friends out of some of those folks.

I can only imagine how hard it is for millions of Americans to live with the conflict that exists between their social and political views, and the multi-cultural experiences they actually enjoy. It must be difficult to enjoy the offerings of people from different ethnic groups while maintaining hostilities toward those same people.

Unfortunately for such individuals, America is becoming more ethnically and culturally diverse with each passing day.

According to the Census Bureau the Hispanic population in this country increased by thirteen percent between the years 2000 and 2003. The Asian population grew by twelve and a half percent during the same time frame. This rate of growth has significantly outpaced the three percent increase in the overall population in this country during those years, and the trend is expected to continue in the future. Clearly, we are experiencing an ongoing cultural and social change that over time will erode the base that the preservationists wish to hold on to.

Before I leave this subject, I can't help but mention one of my favorite examples of the differentiation game.

The indoor tanning industry in this country grosses over four billion dollars a year. It is estimated that there are over fifty thousand tanning salons across the country, and the number is growing. Thousands of people use these salons in spite of the fact that organizations like The Centers for Disease Control and Prevention, American Cancer Society, and Food and Drug Administration are firm in their positions that the ultraviolet rays from both the sun and tanning lamps can cause skin cancer.

In October 2003, Case Western Reserve University released the results of a study conducted with approximately seven thousand white teenagers. The study found that forty-seven percent of the eighteen and nineteen-year-old girls surveyed have used tanning booths at least three times. As they get older, these teenagers will become the customer base that will support these establishments in the future, in spite of the medical risks.

I can't remember how many times a co-worker would go to the beach during the weekend, and make a point of finding me when we were back in the office to compare their tan to my skin color. "Roll up your sleeve. Ooh, I'm as dark as you are," is the typical line that I have heard.

Now I suppose that I was to take their comment as a compliment. However, in reality it was typically nothing more than an irritant. I would generally wonder why they would want to look like me and at the same time not want to go to lunch with me. Ever.

Quite honestly, these folks ultimately proved to be more amusing than irritating. Half of the time they tanned with their sunglasses on, and looked like Rocky the Raccoon from the Bullwinkle Moose cartoons. Their skin was so fried that they were peeling, and walking slower than my one hundred-and-two-year-old neighbor in her orthopedic shoes, unable to either sit down or stand up without grimacing in pain. But boy it was great to look like me!

Take a stroll through a shopping mall sometime. Look closely at who is wearing a Beyonce' teeshirt, carrying hip-hop CD's in her bag, and sporting a sun lamp tan to boot. And yet we want to play the same old differentiation games. Imagine that.

Chapter 22

We Love Our High Profile Hypocrites!

I was recently talking to a friend of mine about the drug use epidemic in this country. We both agreed that the use of illegal drugs and abuse of prescription drugs is a major social concern. We also agreed that illicit drug use needs to be addressed on a very serious level.

Visualize the following scenario, and ask yourself how the typical highly principled person in this country would expect the situation to be addressed if he or she were directly involved.

Like millions of Americans, you report to your place of employment, run by a very powerful boss who happens to be a condescending loudmouth. However, in spite of his personality, you and the boss generally get along well.

Your boss is aware that your spouse sustained an injury from a fall, and he asks you how he or she is feeling and if they are taking any pain medication. When you respond with a 'yes' your boss asks you if your spouse can spare a few of his or her OxyContin painkiller pills. I would imagine that you would begin to feel just a little bit of pressure, but you decide to supply him with a few pills, hoping he will never ask you again.

However, a few pills is only the beginning.

At your bosses threatening insistence, you begin to provide him with up to ten pills a day. And when your spouse's doctor stops renewing the prescription, your boss threatens you by telling you that you'd *better* find a different way to get him more pills.

So you find an illegitimate supplier, and routinely hide the pills in a place where no one else can find them. By now you are hiding up to eighty pills a day! You even secretively meet with your boss in parking lots to exchange sandwich bags filled with pills for money. This relationship continues for a period of four years. Subsequently you leave your job but continue to supply your now ex-boss with pills at his insistence.

A few years later, despite having tacitly agreed to remain silent while your boss was 'paying you off', you decide to report him or her to the authorities, and they begin an investigation.

Wouldn't you feel that this drug abuser should be strongly dealt with by the legal authorities? This person bullied a subordinate to supply him or her with pills that were not prescribed for them, and to engage themselves with a drug ring in order to keep the supply channel open. And all along the subordinate was paid to keep the pills coming and his or her mouth shut. This scenario sounds highly unethical and quite possibly illegal to me. Most people would be shocked and appalled you say?

Now I would fully expect that someone like, oh, Rush Limbaugh, the media voice for the ultra-conservative right wing sect of this country, would agree as well. Mr. Limbaugh is the mouthpiece of the self proclaimed, highly moralistic, self righteous, and holier-than-thou Americans.

You know the type. They are highly critical of liberals and apologists for the conservatives. In their minds the social issues in this country are *never* about politics, race or economics. In their view it's always about personal drive and responsibility which, in their opinion, are the only variables that count for making it in America.

But wait a minute. Something just dawned on me. Mr. Limbaugh *couldn't* agree.

Why?

Because the 'OxyContin pill popping, blackmailing, bullying, threatening the supplier, hiding the pills from sight and buying them in the parking lot' guy is Rush Limbaugh!

I've heard that we should all be held to the same standards in this society. Let's see how this played out.

I thought that Mr. Rush Limbaugh's position on illicit drug use was crystal clear. Back in 1995, he was quoted as saying, "Too many whites are getting away with drug use. The answer is to find the ones who are getting away with it, convict them, and send them up the river."

I have heard him disparage people time and time again about personal responsibility. For example, he made Darryl Strawberry, the ex-major league baseball player, his whipping boy when Strawberry had a drug abuse problem.

'OxyContin Rush' preaches that there should be absolute consequences for breaking the rules, and that the rule of law in this county is much too lenient because of 'bleeding heart' liberals who pander to the immoral and the lawless.

Given this position on issues of right and wrong, I have been waiting patiently for his twenty million-listener audience to initiate a movement to have him 'sent up the river'. So far I haven't seen anything that I can put my finger on indicating that the movement has begun.

I know how his legion of supporters feels because I have heard their views time again about drug users and their suppliers, typically in reference to 'inner city' folks who are active in the illegal drug trade - you know, the folks who are referred to as 'law-breaking low lives' who have no morals and sell drugs. According to these folks, the customers who buy and use the drugs are equally as guilty for their actions, and should do jail time at the very least.

And as for rehabilitation you ask?

Well, the 'OxyContin Rush' faithful doesn't think that rehab is the answer. In their minds, drug suppliers and users are criminals who *choose* to abuse drugs. Rehab is viewed as too lenient and would simply play into the abusers' hands by giving them a 'get out of jail free card'.

Teach them all a lesson - suppliers and users alike - put them in jail!

Given that position I'd like to know how much jail time good ole' Rush will be serving? No, I didn't say "Russ", the kid from the ghetto who is in a holding cell because he is suspected (but not convicted) of trafficking drugs. Not "Ross", the drug user who would like to go to rehab but is being made an example of by the court system. I said Rush, as in Rush Limbaugh!

Last I heard he did a few weeks of rehab, and quietly went back to doing his radio show. In the process, he became a sympathetic figure for his supporters. I guess that's a good thing. I would fully expect that from now on 'OxyContin Rush' and his followers will demonstrate incredible compassion for drug addicts. So stay tuned...but don't get your hopes up.

I can just imagine the consequences that *I* would face if I attempted to turn a subordinate in the workplace to my own personal drug supplier. Going to jail would be the least of my problems. I would probably be on the news, with handcuffs on, a jacket over my head, branded the scourge of our society.

And on my way to jail I would probably be thinking to myself, "Gee, if I were only born a self-proclaimed ultra-conservative loudmouth blowhard with twenty million people who listen to me on the radio..."

But it's not about the 'what' it's about the 'who'. It's not about justice it's about wealth and power.

We love our high profile hypocrites because the fundamental culture of this society is rooted in hypocrisy. Mr. Limbaugh is representative of many Americans who talk about treating everyone by the same rules and standards. What they fail to add is 'as long that those rules and standards do not have to apply to them personally'.

The self-proclaimed, highly ethical, highly moral conservatives in this country can be as transparent as they come. The art of talking one game and playing another appears to be the course of action for many of them, especially when it comes to their *own* personal accountability and integrity.

More recently 'OxyContin Rush' took shots at Bill Clinton after the release of *My Life*, the former president's memoirs about his life and years in the White House. Limbaugh referred to the book as *My Lie*, because of Clinton's dishonesty when he went through the impeachment process during the Monica Lewinsky scandal.

It should amaze me that Limbaugh would take such a position about Clinton - 'OxyContin Rush' was exposed for being an incredible hypocrite, as well as closet prescription drug abuser. But it doesn't.

Bill Clinton lied about his personal life, which was fundamentally a family matter. However, without question he should have been held to the highest moral standard as the President of this country. Limbaugh forced an employee to get pills for him through illegal channels. Neither act was of a high moral standard, but there is a difference between them. Arguably Limbaugh *broke the law* and Clinton didn't.

203

So for 'Oxycontin Rush' to take shots at Bill Clinton is the height of hypocrisy.

In addition, the Limbaughs of the world have always had a lot to say about Bill and Hillary Clinton's relationship. The fact is, despite everything that was made public about the Clinton's relationship and marital issues, they are still together. I believe that 'OxyContin Rush' and much of the holier-than-thou crowd are hypocrites for having so much to say about their marriage.

But I may be wrong.

'OxyContin Rush' just might be an expert on the subject of marriage. Surely he has had enough practice to develop his expertise. In fact, during the timeframe that Clinton released his book Limbaugh's wife had filed for a divorce, which will be the *third* divorce for the voice of family values. So much for 'OxyContin Rush' having any credibility on the subject of relationships.

I can't help but add that his last wedding was hosted *and* officiated by none other than Supreme Court Justice Clarence Thomas. Limbaugh should have known that anything Thomas touches ultimately yields bad results -black folks certainly do.

I get tired of listening to the conservative holier-than-thou crowd in this country preach about personal responsibility, morality and opportunity. Don't misunderstand me. I believe very strongly in all of these things. But when I turn on the news, I get my daily dose of George Bush's war, the Enron, WorldCom, and Tyco corporate scandals, the Martha Stewart's case, the Governor of Connecticut's impeachment, and the sex abuse scandal in the Catholic Church and other such hypocrisy all in one thirty minute broadcast.

So much for practicing what we preach.

Chapter 23

Hypocrites - The All-Time Champion

Let's move on to the all-time champion, the all-time king, and the ultimate American symbol of hypocrisy. The winner of this dubious award is none other than the Honorable Senator from South Carolina, the late Strom Thurmond!

Strom Thurmond - another great American hero. So great and honorable a man was he that *his* secret didn't come out until six months after his death. It's a shame he didn't live long enough to publicly face up to what he really was.

Yes, I'm talking about Strom 'The Two-Faced Hypocrite' Thurmond, henceforth to be referred to as 'Sham' Thurmond. For over eighty years he was a major force in the fight to preserve segregation and the pillars of racism in this country. 'Sham' was an opponent to anyone involved in the fight for civil rights and equality in education, employment and housing opportunities for all Americans.

205

'Sham' was born and raised in South Carolina, and was so strong in his beliefs that in 1948 he ran for President on the segregationist platform, leading the movement to preserve discrimination. During one of his campaign speeches he stated to an audience of his supporters, "I wanna tell you, ladies and gentlemen, that there's not enough troops in the army to force the southern people to break down segregation and admit the nigger race into our theaters, into our swimming pools, into our homes, and into our churches."

What 'Sham' failed to tell that audience, and the rest of the world for that matter, was that at precisely the same moment he was the father of a twenty-three year old black woman!!

Yes, in the tradition of Thomas Jefferson and others like him, the new king of the white separatists had sexual relations with a *black* woman *and* fathered a child with her under the cover of secrecy.

Given that 'Sham' was the sham that he was, I bet that he led a double life. He probably bought into the stereotypes that were and continued to be perpetuated about the 'typical' black male in this society.

I bet that when good ole' 'Sham' got home from work after a hard day of figuring out new and creative ways to discriminate against black people, the real person came out of the closet. I can picture him taking off his shirt and tie, peeling the press-on confederate flag tattoo from his forearm, and heading for the living room sofa. He would put on a James Brown album (his favorite artist), and sing 'Hot Pants' while dancing on the living room carpet.

Sometime later in the evening, he would go upstairs and change into a red crushed velvet suit with a black shirt opened down to his navel and hang a gold chain around his neck. Then he would put on a matching red brim and gator shoes, and slip on a pinky ring. After checking himself out in the mirror, 'Sham' would head down to the club and party the night away, drinking straight whiskey with a toothpick in his mouth and flirting with the ladies. All of the time looking like a fool since, contrary to the stereotype, black folks don't come equipped with a pimp wardrobe starter kit. And all of the time denying to himself and the rest of the world the existence of Essie Mae, his black daughter.

Essie Mae Washington is the seventy-eight year old daughter of 'Sham'. He was twenty-two when he fathered her with Carrie Butler, a sixteen-year-old domestic working for his family. Ms. Washington did not meet her *upstanding* father until she was sixteen years old, and since that time lived with his secret. 'Sham' saw to it that she always received money from him, and they shared clandestine visits and routinely sent cards and letters to each other.

Let's see. On the one hand 'Sham' and Essie Mae Washington had to *hide* that she is the daughter of a prominent white man, but on the other hand we are to believe that this country doesn't have a race problem.

What a joke.

Public knowledge of 'Sham's' black daughter would have been a major problem for him. I cannot imagine how difficult it had to be for her knowing that her own father could not publicly acknowledge her existence without him feeling shamed, embarrassed and humiliated.

After the revelation of Ms. Washington's history, the public and the media, in typical fashion, attempted to reshape the entire story. As black people in this country, we have seen this phenomenon time and time again. Rather than deal with their hero 'Sham' for what he was, which was a race-baiting hypocrite, they attempted to transform him into a loving father who provided emotional and financial support to his daughter.

The story sounds like the transformation of several of our forefathers - race-baiting hypocrites turned into heroes.

'Sham' has been portrayed as a caring father who looked out for the well-being of his daughter. We've been told he loved his daughter and grandchildren, but chose to keep their existence secret in *both* of their best interests.

Both of their interests?

This would imply that *she* had as much to lose as he did if her story came out. Oh really? A white separatist southern senator who's crusade for segregation shaped his political existence and influenced national race relations and politics having a black child, *versus* the child who comes into the world with no personal history at stake or a need to keep a secret. This doesn't quite sound like an equal risk of exposure to me.

We all know why she was kept a secret until his death. *American history has taught us that if you can't undo the truth about the past, you hide it or create another version that will make us feel good.*

I also heard that 'Sham' was proud of his daughter. Well, where was she at his 100th birthday party – sitting in the front row?

There is another aspect of this story that was conveniently glossed over. 'Sham' had sexual relations with a fifteen-year-old girl! The last time that I checked, having sexual relations with a fifteen-year-old minor was both illegal and morally reprehensible. What would have been the political cost to him because of his relationship with a fifteen-year-old girl?

I know that I am regressing, but somehow I get the feeling that 'OxyContin Rush' Limbaugh learned to play the game of 'our little secret' from Mr. Thurmond. They are both cut from the same transparent cloth of ultra-conservative moralists full of bravado masking the hypocrisy with which they conduct their lives. They are not unlike the typical moralist that I have heard of or encountered in this country.

I know, 'Sham's' sham was a highly unique case. There wasn't much race mixing back in the good ole' days of blatant segregation.

Sure.

So help me understand? How did we become a society comprised of people, both white and black, whose skin tones and facial and other characteristics run across an incredibly wide spectrum? Obviously, *somebody* was mixing the pool long before there was any widespread acceptance in doing so.

Too many folks chose to act as if integration and 'race mixing' is a reasonably new phenomenon. And some actually believe that they began in earnest after the civil rights movement with the passage of laws fostering the integration of public places and educational systems, and the implementation of fair employment and housing laws.

The reality of American history is that the beginning of the 'mixing of the races' was, at the very least, three hundred and fifty years ago! And it wasn't exactly at the choosing of the Native Americans and African slaves. It began with the settlers and the Thomas Jeffersons of the world, men with power over blacks and other minorities in their respective eras who fathered children with members of the very groups that they actively enslaved and/or discriminated against.

The 'problems' didn't begin until our ancestors began to demand and fight for human rights and equality under the law, and dared step over the still visible line in this country.

The distinction that I draw is a simple one. Integration with blacks and Native Americans was fine with white folks as long as terms like *'human rights'* and *'equality under the law'* weren't in the picture. It was only when the demands for human rights and equality under the law began that things started to change.

Unfortunately, they haven't changed enough.

Chapter 24

Sweet Home, Alabama

Since I am on the subject of moralists, I have to say that the only thing worse than an *individual* hypocrite is a *state* that has gone on record as being such, like the great state of Alabama.

Alabama was at the forefront of the battles over segregation as recently as the civil rights movements of the 1960's. The city of Birmingham was widely known as 'Bombingham' because of the more than fifty occasions of blacks having their homes and other properties bombed between 1948 and 1965.

On a Sunday morning in September of 1963, Birmingham's Sixteen Street Baptist Church was bombed in a racially motivated crime. Four black girls were killed. The bombing was an attempt to intimidate blacks who had won a federal court order to integrate Birmingham's schools. Despite the continued acts of intimidation, the schools were eventually desegregated.

Alabama's history also included a famous protest against racism in 1963 that was met with strong resistance. Dogs and fire hoses were turned on the protesters by the city's police department, and subsequent protests included the beating of demonstrators in the city of Selma in 1964. Ultimately, the national spotlight thrown on Alabama led to major national legislation such as the Civil Rights Act of 1964 and the Voting Rights Act of 1965.

Let's fast forward to the year 2001.

During that summer, Alabama Chief Justice Roy Moore, in his infinite wisdom, decided that a two-ton granite monument of the Ten Commandments should be moved into the state courthouse rotunda. After careful planning, he had the monument moved into the courthouse in the middle of the night. I can only imagine that since the state of Alabama is a model of Christian values in our society - among them being brotherly love - such an act on his part was quite reasonable.

The Justice's decision resulted in lawsuits being filed by the American Civil Liberties Union and the Americans United for Separation in a fight to enforce the laws of the separation of church and state, which is the belief that the government should not attempt to integrate religion into governmental affairs.

Sounds good to me. Religion has been used in America as a *justification* for discrimination against select groups of people.

Going back in history, the settlers cited, among other things, their religious beliefs as the basis for converting those *lost* Native Americans to their culture (they also used a little technique called annihilation as a means of conversion). The Ku Klux Klan has also used religion as their basis for hating everybody.

The mantra 'In God We Trust' has been used in this country as the basis for everything from war to the practice of discrimination based on religion and/or sexual orientation. When in doubt we refer to the mantra – Americans just can't get enough of it.

In December 2002, Judge Moore received an ultimatum from the federal court to remove the statute from the courthouse, but was also given the opportunity to appeal the ruling. In the meantime, his position created a groundswell of support among the moral sect. They asked

211

the questions 'Why shouldn't the statute stay in the courthouse? Isn't God the pillar of our society? Etc., etc.'

Subsequently, a federal judge ordered that the monument be removed, and it was taken from the courthouse in August of 2003. Judge Moore was also removed from his position for resisting the order. In addition, his vow to fight for the integration of Christian values into government was met with a plan by the Southern Poverty Law Center (SPLC) to petition the Alabama State Bar Association to have him disbarred. This is the same SPLC that monitors the over seven-hundred hate groups that are still alive in this country, many of whom are situated in the holier-than-thou state of Alabama.

But wait. It gets more interesting.

Alabama just happens to be the *last* state in this country to change their law banning interracial marriage, which remained illegal in that state until 2001! In reality, the U.S. Supreme Court had ruled in 1967 that such bans couldn't be enforced by any state. However, the symbolism that existed in Alabama spoke volumes. In the entire state only one white legislator, Attorney General Bill Pryor, would even support a ballot measure for public vote in the state.

The most telling part of this issue was that the measure passed in a statewide vote by a margin of fifty-nine percent to forty-one percent! Forty-one percent of the voters came out *against* interracial marriage.

So here's my point of confusion.

I cannot figure out how a population of people can *support* having a statute of the Ten Commandments in its state courthouse rotunda under the "In God We Trust' mantra, and at the same time have forty-one percent of its voters come out *against* interracial marriage.

Isn't God the God of all people? Aren't we all brothers and sisters in this colorblind society? Obviously not. But I'm not the least bit surprised. I would bet, without reservation, that Alabama is not unique in this regard.

I would love to see how a secret vote in each of the fifty states would turn out, and if the forty-percent or more opposed benchmark would hold up.

If you could ask the typical American how they feel about this issue they would probably *tell* you that they would have no problem with people marrying or socializing with whomever they chose to. They would emphatically state that they have no hang-ups regarding this issue. You know, they have friends who have friends... That is, until its time to vote their conscience in secrecy, where no one can see them. Then the story would probably be different.

Hypocrisy is most comfortable when practiced in the safety of anonymity.

'NIMBY' is a phrase which means 'not in my backyard'. It is commonly used by communities in response to a government's or business' plans to build something like a power plant or prison. It generally means 'I'm OK with whatever you do as long as it doesn't involve me, affect me or require me to see or live near it'. NIMBY" is played on a much larger scale with issues affecting our daily lives:

- Should the disadvantaged have access to good quality affordable housing? Yes, but NIMBY

- Should all children have access to a good quality education? Yes, but NIMBY

- Should everyone who meets the qualifications be afforded equal opportunity to job advancement? Yes, but NIMBY

- Should gay or lesbian couples be allowed to live as a family? Maybe, but NIMBY

- Should gay priests be allowed to marry another male? Never and NIMBY! (This issue is particularly interesting. As a priest you can seduce, molest, and sodomize young men, and be *treated* to a transfer to another parish full of other young men to continue your behavior if you get caught. Better yet, your leadership will attempt to silence the victims with a financial payoff, and you will never face jail time like a mere mortal citizen. In a nutshell, you can sexually abuse young men…you just can't marry them!).

I am so used to seeing and hearing examples of this stuff that I named my dog NIMBY! That way I'll never lose sight of how the game is really played.

Chapter 25

So Why Are You Mad At Me?

I can imagine that there are people who cannot understand how a survivor of the World Trade Center attack could possibly have the views that I do about both our government and society in general. They would probably expect me to simply be blindly patriotic after personally experiencing such a brutal act.

And I can imagine that there are folks who would take the position that "America is the greatest country on earth. If I don't like it, why don't I leave?"

We've all heard it before - the predictably simple and mindless response to any level of criticism of this country or perceived lack of blind patriotism.

Well, for those folks I am always happy to answer the question: *Part of my ancestry was here for thousands of years before the friendly settlers arrived. The other part of my ancestry was dragged over on slave ships in chains to provide a little free labor for the settlers and their descendants.*

So this land *is* home. I'm not going anywhere!

And come to think of it, I've never hurt anyone. I'm an upstanding, law abiding citizen who treats people with respect. So I would pose the following question:

Why are you mad at me?

215

- I didn't highjack airplanes and use them to destroy the World Trade Center.

- I didn't make a conscious effort to kill thousands of people in a vicious attack.

- I don't run the agencies that spend billions of tax dollars on defense initiatives but were totally unprepared to protect us from such an attack.

- I didn't send your kids to war - at a cost of over one billion dollars a week - with the false justification that Iraq posed imminent danger, and possessed weapons of mass destruction.

- I didn't stand on the USS Lincoln, dressed in a fighter pilot suit like a super hero, declaring that the war in Iraq was over and claiming victory, only to have hundreds of soldiers killed and thousands injured after my show of bravado.

- I haven't spent billions of dollars on intelligence efforts only to have to admit to the world that the intelligence that I allegedly used to justify going to war was wrong.

- I haven't driven the U.S. Treasury from surplus to a level of debt unprecedented in the history of this country, in large part because of war related expenditures.
- I haven't raised your taxes and wasted your tax dollars while cutting services and ignoring our country's education systems, crumbling highways and deteriorating railroads.

- I didn't make the cost of medical insurance and prescription drugs so expensive that you can't afford them.

- I haven't driven the price of a gallon of gasoline to the highest level in history making it so expensive that you have to decide which meal to skip in order to afford the trip to work.

- I haven't lined my pockets with millions of dollars while serving as one of your company's top executives, and then either laid you off, raided or destroyed your pensions and retirement programs.

- I didn't move jobs overseas to cut expenses and maximize profits while putting you out of work, and contributed to two million people losing their jobs in less than a two-year period of time.

- I didn't cut unemployment benefits for people who are unemployed in the middle of a terrible job market.

- I'm not responsible for the record number of real estate foreclosures and personal bankruptcies filed by Americans during the last few years.

- I haven't made it easy for people to walk into a national department store and buy a rifle or gun that they saw advertised in a sales circular.

- I'm not the reason that you fear letting your own children walk home from school or go to the grocery store by themselves.

- I'm not the one who made it easy for children and adults to get a hold of prescription drugs from mail order or cyberspace drug dealers.

- I haven't made it possible for children to purchase alcohol on the Internet without their parents' knowledge.

- I don't design or sell violent videogames, or create Internet sites that have helped turn violence into a competitive sport for a growing population of people.

- I don't write and produce the television programs that promote violence and personal irresponsibility to your children.

- I don't market food products to children and young adults that contribute to the childhood obesity epidemic and increasing rates of juvenile diabetes in this country.

- I didn't make the determination that our society is better served by spending an estimated sixty thousand dollars a year to incarcerate a prisoner, while only spending six thousand dollars a year to educate a student.

- I haven't created an economic system where the educators who teach our children are amongst the lowest paid professionals, while the lawyers who are paid to defend our children in the legal system are among the highest paid professionals.

- I haven't made the political arena such a turn off that Americans would rather vote for a singer on *American Idol* than vote in a political election.

- I haven't poisoned our streams to the point where eating seafood in certain parts of the country is a calculated risk.

- I didn't get you excited about the new wave of miracle pills that will do everything from increase your vitality to help you shed pounds without dieting or exercising, only to have you find out that there are side effects like... bad breath, hair loss, tooth decay, crossed eyes, hammer toes, acne, claustrophobia, amnesia, insomnia, arthritis, bursitis, dementia, runny nose, ringing in the ears, swollen lips, tennis elbow, dandruff, sore throat, swollen glands, foot odor, hiccupping, belching, passing gas, hallucinations, delusions of grandeur, memory loss, sucking your thumb, slurred speech, and rabies…all from taking a single pill.

So why be mad at me?

Chapter 26

A Day In The City

I was in Manhattan the other day, and I paid a visit to the World Trade Center site.

As I stood on Church Street looking at the site through the fence, the events of September 11, 2001 came back to me in vivid detail. I remembered how it felt being in the stairwell trying to get to the bottom of the north tower, the chaos on the mezzanine as people looked out at the bodies and devastation on the plaza, and how the north tower became completely dark and smoke filled. I also remembered running up West Street just before the towers collapsed.

The most chilling recollection was of the screaming and crying that I heard during the worst moments of the ordeal; crawling around on the north tower mezzanine after the south tower collapsed, and seeing the bodies on the plaza.

As I stood there I also thought about how, in an ironic sense, the world was *different* on that day.

In a time of life threatening danger, race was not an issue. People that I didn't know took direction from me with no questions asked. They didn't avoid eye contact or walk in another direction, or stand in place and contemplate whether they should follow my lead. And they didn't ask to see my identification or speak to my supervisor. Survival was the only thought on our collective minds.

I also started thinking that, other than the predictable treatment of folks from the Middle East, there was an incredible sense of *unity* we all exhibited during the crisis.

From my perspective the level of civility among us all of us had noticeably improved. For a moment in time divisive issues like race and religion really didn't seem to matter, and there was a tangible sense of genuine concern for people around us.

It was a good feeling.

I imagine that given my perspectives about history and today's world there are people who would feel that I am entirely unpatriotic. Nothing is further from the truth.

The fact that I am an American has provided me with the freedom to put my perspectives on paper without seeking anyone's approval, and without fear of being punished by a disapproving government.

I firmly believe that the ability to take advantage of the opportunities offered in this country is a birthright that comes with citizenship. And fortunately for me, I have had the opportunity, resources and support needed to do so. This is my home. I would not choose to live anywhere else. However, not all of us are as fortunate as I am.

I recognize that as Americans we have freedoms and resources that are unavailable to millions of people around the world. This is the richest and most powerful country on the globe. Many people from other countries look to make America their home, and come here to take advantage of what it has to offer.

As Americans we have the freedom to practice our choice of religion, and exercise our political beliefs as well as freedom of speech.

We have the freedom of movement, and the ability to visit and experience the natural beauty of this nation, ranging from the incredible cities across the country to the mountains, rivers, and wide-open spaces.

Our education system provides opportunities to learn at all levels, and our medical institutions offer the most advanced practices and technologies in the world.

But we are by no means the perfect society.

I thought about the notion that in this day and age, too many Americans still have issues with people who do not fit their definition of '*us*'.

And I asked myself '*what is us?*' In a country with citizens from hundreds of nations around the world, what is the definitive '*us*'?

With so many people who are multi-racial and multi-lingual, what is the singular '*us*' that so many Americans are trying to hold on to?

It's about time that we collectively wake up, end the separation games, and move on with life.

Ironically, I was standing in Manhattan, the heart of the most multi-cultural city in the world, and as I stood there an example of how race games are *still* played in the New York area and in this country came to mind. During the week of my visit to the World Trade Center site, a study conducted by the Association of Community Organizations for Reform Now (ACORN) in Nassau County, New York (which borders New York City to the east) had discovered rampant discrimination practices in apartment rentals.

According to ACORN, one hundred sixty-four testers, seventy-nine white and eighty-five who were either black or Hispanic, all with very similar economic profiles, inquired about renting apartments through sixteen real estate companies in the community.

Twelve of the companies steered blacks and Hispanics away from predominantly white communities by telling them that no rentals were available in their price range.

Overall, the study determined that agents offered to show apartments to seventy-four percent of the white testers, as opposed to thirty-three percent of the minority testers.

Sadly enough, some of those minority 'testers' could have been former or current soldiers in the military committed to fighting to protect the lives and freedoms of the very Long Islanders who would not even show them an apartment.

And I asked myself again, in reality, what has been the lasting impact of 9/11 on race relations in America?

After a while, I said my mental good-byes to the World Trade Center site, and walked over to the Fulton Street Station on Broadway. I got on the same subway that I had ridden hundreds of times before to Grand Central Terminal. This trip was only the second that I had taken from that location to Grand Central Terminal since September 11th.

I rode the subway thinking how good it was to have been back to the site, and to have had the chance to reminisce about what it was like to work at the World Trade Center for sixteen years.

When I arrived at Grand Central Terminal, I ran across the concourse to catch my train home. I got on the train and sat down with only three minutes to spare.

And on the way back to Connecticut the world around me snapped me back to reality. The hypocrisies and contradictions that are America reared their heads once again.

I sat by myself all of the way home...

It was just another day in 'color blind' America...

Some walls just don't want to fall...

223

EPILOGUE

There are several significant pieces of legislation that have been passed during the last fifty years. Among them are two that have provided the framework for improving the quality of life for all Americans.

In 1954, the case of *Brown vs. the Board of Education,* which was in regard to the appropriateness of segregation in public education, was decided by the United States Supreme Court in a landmark decision. The court ruled that segregation in public schools was unconstitutional. This decision led the way for the desegregation of public schools across the country on a large scale.

Linda Brown was a black third grade student who had to walk approximately one mile to her elementary school in Topeka, Kansas in the early 1950's. On her way, she would pass a white elementary school that was only seven or eight blocks away from her home. Consequently, her father, Oliver Brown, attempted to enroll her in the local elementary school, but had his request denied by the school's principal.

In 1951, Mr. Brown, supported by the Topeka branch of the National Association for the Advancement of Colored People (NAACP), requested that the United States District Court for the District of Kansas stop the practice of segregation in the school system. He maintained that the existence of segregated schools generated feelings of inferiority among black children.

After hearing the case, the court ultimately upheld the segregation policy, largely based on the *Plessy vs. Ferguson* decision in 1896, which established the principle of "separate but equal" for public schools. The court took the position that since the Supreme Court had not overturned the separate but equal statute it would not force the Topeka Board of Education to do so.

The case was appealed to the Supreme Court in combination with similar cases regarding school segregation practices in Delaware, South Carolina, and Virginia. Thurgood Marshall, who went on to become a Supreme Court Justice, presented it to the court. Marshall argued that there was no valid reason for segregation, and that the practice of separate but equal facilities caused psychological damage to black children. He also argued that the practice violated the 14th Amendment, which provided equal protection under the law.

The Supreme Court ultimately ruled in favor of Brown in 1954. It asked, "Does segregation of children in public schools solely on the base of race, even though the physical facilities...may be equal, deprive the children of the minority group of equal opportunities?" The court concluded that it did, and that, "in the field of public education the doctrine of separate but equal has no place." The court also stated that segregation was unconstitutional under the 14th Amendment.

In my view, that Supreme Court decision was the single most important piece of legislation passed in the 20th century. It fundamentally changed the way that Americans lived their lives, and began the momentum for other legislation, like the Civil Rights Act of 1964, which was aimed at ending segregation. The integration of public schools was the entry point to desegregation.

About a decade later, Congress passed the Voting Rights Act of 1965, which was signed into law by President Lyndon Johnson. This act eliminated requirements such as the ability to pass literacy tests and pay poll usage taxes in order to vote. It also attempted to stop the harassment and intimidation of people attempting to register to vote. As a result of this act, the number of registered voters within black and other minority communities increased significantly.

Many people fought and died for the right of all Americans to receive a quality education in the public school system. Yet, fifty years later, our public school systems fail to provide an acceptable standard of education to youth who live in primarily urban and rural environments. Our public schools are failing us.

It appears that our priorities in this society are in the wrong place. For example, in the past twenty years approximately two-thirds of the thirty major league baseball franchises have opened brand new stadiums, many of which involved some level of public financing.

We can spend billions of dollars on baseball stadiums for millionaire athletes and billionaire owners to make money, but we can't find resources to ensure that our children receive a quality education?

I strongly believe that we have both an *opportunity* and a *responsibility* to make sure that the expressed intent of the education and voting legislation becomes the priority that it needs to be. We all have a right to a quality education, and we need to progress an agenda that fosters that right. Education on all levels is the key to the future of our society, and it must take place in both an academic and social context.

The academic component ensures that children will grow up with the skills and abilities to qualify for the types of employment opportunities that will enable them to provide for themselves and their families. They will also be able to understand the political and economic factors that affect their lives, and be prepared to handle the day-to-day challenges that they will face.

The social component ensures that people from different backgrounds learn how to interact comfortably with each other. This skill is fostered in environments where such social interaction is ongoing. Typically, school systems are the first point of contact for children of diverse backgrounds. Everyone needs to develop the social skills and perspectives needed to function respectfully and successfully in our society.

We must ensure that all voices are heard, and the best place to start is in the political arena, which offers the ability to effect large scale change. Each and every one of us who is eligible has a *responsibility* to vote! Our votes in local, state, and federal elections will determine the course of our country's future.

We need to understand that presidential elections are particularly critical, not simply because of the important role of the president, but also because every president creates a lasting legacy by virtue of their appointments to the United States Supreme Court during their presidency.

For example, the composition of the Supreme Court was the determining factor in the outcome of the 2000 *Florida* election, and thus the *presidential* election. If the Supreme Court had allowed the recount in Florida to take place, George Bush would not have assumed the presidency.

State and local elections are equally important. In addition to electing our politicians we vote on referendums that determine how our tax dollars are spent in our communities. A strong voice in the voting process can influence the decisions that are made about how to spend money for needs like improvements to our school or transportation systems (as opposed to whether we need public financing for a new ball field, skating ring, or public golf course).

227

We also have the ability to effect change economically. As a consumer, if you are not happy with a particular company or retailer, don't purchase their products, and don't frequent their establishments.

We enjoy many freedoms in this country. Among them is the ability to get an education as well as the right to vote. Education means empowerment, and with empowerment comes the opportunity to enjoy a good quality of life.

So exercise your freedom.

Demand a good education!

And make sure that you vote!

BIBLIOGRAPHY

· ABC News. "Fear and Relief (Jessica Lynch)"; November 11, 2003

· AOL News. "Powell Not Sure Iraq Trailers Were Labs"; April 3, '04

· Adelante On Line. "Tens of Thousands of Americans Commemorating Martin Luther King Day"; Jan 20, 2004

· Angle, Jim, Wendell Goler and Liza Porteus. "State of the Union Address Focuses on Iraq, Economy, Path Ahead", FOX News; January 21, 2004

· Aita, Judy. "U.S. Presents Iraq Disarmament Draft Resolution to Security Council", United States Mission to the European Union; October 23, 2002

· Ananova. "Civil Rights Commission Says Florida Election Was Unfair to Blacks"; June 5, 2001

· Armas, Genaro. "Hispanic, Asian Populations Still Growing", Associated Press; June 14, 2004

· Associated Press. "Bush Puts Pickering on Appeals Court"; January 16, 2004

· Associated Press. "Bush's WMD Jokes Draw Criticism"; March 26, 2004

· Associated Press. "France Calls Emergency U.N. Meeting Tuesday"; March 17, 2003

· Associated Press. "Many Teens Still Get Indoor Tans"; October 31, 2003

· BarnesandNoble.com."The Politics of Truth"; Joseph Wilson; 5/04

· BBC News. "Florida's Black Voters Protest"; January 11, 2001

· BET.com. "Black Army Specialist is One of Five Prisoners of War"; March 23, 2003

· BET.com. "Women at War"; April 2, 2003

· Begleiter, Ralph. "George Bush Says He Could Have Done More to Oust Saddam Hussein", CNN; January 16, 1996

· Benedetto, Richard. "Poll: Most Back War, But Want U.N. Support"; USA Today; March 16, 2003

· Benge, George. "Formal, Private Tributes Honor Fallen Native American Soldier", Gannett News Service; May 8, 2003

· BlackElectorate.com. "Africa and Aboriginal Tuesdays: Inside the Dispute Between the State of New York and the Seneca Nation"; January 20, 2004

· Bowman, John. "In-Depth: Timothy McVeigh", CBC News;
    May 2000
· Brown, Mitchell (Compiler). "Martin Luther King Jr.
    Chronology", LSU Libraries; December 11, 2003
· Brown, Nathan (Contributor). "Persian Gulf War", MSN Encarta;
    1997-2004
· Bugliosi, Vincent. "Betrayal of America: How the Supreme
    Court Undermined the Constitution and Chose Our
    President", Thunder's Mouth Press; 2001
· CBC News. "Five Years Later, 168 Bombing Victims Honored";
    April 19, 2000
· CBS News. "Bush, Chirac Talk Iraq to U.N."; September 23, 2003
· CBS News. "Bush: I Want Iraq WMD 'Facts'"; February 2, 2004
· CBS News. "Bush Sought 'Way' to Invade Iraq?"; January 11, 2004
· CBS News. "Strom's Daughter: A Burden Lifted", 60 Minutes II;
    December 18, 2003
· CBSNews.com. "Clarke's Take on Terror"; March 21, 2004
· CBSNews.com. "Woodward Shares War Secrets"; April 18, 2004
· CNN.com. "1999 Year In Review - Massacre at Columbine
    High School Tops a Year of Bloody Headlines"; 2001
· CNN.com. "Alabama Repeals Century-Old Ban on
    Interracial Marriages"; November 8, 2000
· CNN.com. "Bush Camp Tries to Halt Florida Recounts";
    December 9, 2000
· CNN.com. "Bush: Iraq, al Qaeda Linked"; January 30, 2003
· CNN.com. "Bush Names New Civil Administrator"; May 6, 2003
· CNN.com. "Commander in Chief Lands on USS Lincoln"; May
2,'03
· CNN.com. "Florida Supreme Court Won't Throw Out Absentee
    Ballots"; December 1, 2000
· CNN.com. "Former President Bush: 'I Hate Saddam'";
    September 18, 2002
· CNN.com. "In-Depth Specials: The Execution of Timothy
    McVeigh"; 2001
· CNN.com. "Iraq Row Rages as Spain Mourns"; December 3, 2003
· CNN.com. "Limbaugh Admits Addition to Pain Medication";
    October 10, 2003
· CNN.com. "POW Planned on Cooking, Not Fighting";
    March 26, 2003

- CNN.com. "Powell and Rice Defend U.S. Basis For War"; February 12, 2004
- CNN.com. "Powell Confronts Iraq at United Nations"; February 5, 2003
- CNN.com. "Senators: Delay Top Tax Cuts to Pay For Rebuilding Iraq, Afghanistan"; September 22, 2003
- CNN.com. "Sharply Divided High Court Stops Florida Recount"; December 10, 2000
- CNN.com "Tenet Defends CIA on Iraq Intelligence"; February 5, 2004
- CNN.com. "Transcript: David Kay at Senate Hearing"; Jan 28, 2004
- CNN.com. "Tuba City Mourns Soldier Killed in Iraq"; April 6, 2003
- CNN.com. "U.S. Supreme Court Reverses Recount Ruling"; December 13, 2000
- CORE-online.org. "The Voting Rights Act of 1965"; 2004
- CORE-online.org. "Brown vs. The Board of Education"; 2004
- Charmingtowns.com. "A Tribute to Senator J. Strom Thurmond"
- Clarke, Richard. "Against All Enemies: Inside America's War on Terror", The Free Press; 2004
- Connor, Tracy. "Breaking News: Rush on the Record", New York Daily News; October 2, 2003
- Cozzens, Lisa. "Brown v. Board of Education", Watson.org; June 29, 1998
- Curry, George. "Republicans Are Trying to 'Fool' Blacks", BlackAmericaToday.com; January 5, 2004
- DeFrank, Thomas. "Bush's War is Personal", New York Daily News; September 28, 2002
- Dershowitz, Alan. "Supreme Injustice: How the Supreme Court Highjacked Election 2000", Oxford University Press; 2002
- Eisler, Kim Isaac. "Revenge of the Pequots", University of Nebraska (Lincoln); 2001
- Encyclopaedia Britannica. "Bush, George"; 1996
- Factmonster.com. "Civil Rights Timeline", Pearson Education; 2000-2003
- Flexner, Allison. "Judge Halts Review of Limbaugh's Medical Records", CNN; December 24, 2003

231

· Foxwoods.com/The Mashantucket Pequots. "Tribal Nation
   History, Timeline of Events, and Mashantucket
   Pequots Come Home"
· Gaskell, Stephanie, Jennifer Fermino, and Andy Soltis.
   "Heroes Rage at WTC Probe", New York Post; May
   19, 2004
· GlobalSecurity.com. "Attacking Iraq - Countdown
   Timeline"; March 19, 2003
· Graham-Harrison. "Spain Unites to Mourn Iraq Dead",
   Reuters; November 30, 2003
· Green, Rick. "A Nation Once Again", The Hartford
   Courant; January 30, 2004
· Hill, Retha. "Sex and Race in the American South",
   MSNBC; December 31, 2003
· Hirschkorn, Phil, Sean Loughlin, Barbara Starr, and Steve
   Turnham. "Bush, Clinton Figures Defend Terrorism
   Policies", CNN.com; March 23, 2004
· HotelEurope.com. "Destination Guides"; 2002
· Hrcr.org. "Brown vs. Board of Education of Topeka,
   Kansas", Human Constitutional Rights; Printed 2004
· Huus, Kari. "Women In Combat", MSNBC; March 26, 2003
· Ibiblio.org. "Europe Claims America"; April 2004
· Indians.org. "Goodbye Columbus", Rocky Mountain News;
   October 8, 1994
· Jackson, Derrick. "Bush in Denial on Florida's Voting
   Scandal", Boston Globe; January 17, 2001
· Jeffrey, Terence. "A True Vision of Civil Rights",
   Townhall.com; June 18, 2003
· Jet Magazine. "Alabama to Vote on Ending Interracial
   Marriage Ban During November Elections"; October
   23, 2000
· Johnson, Bob. "Ousted Judge Doesn't Think He's a
   Martyr", The Associated Press; November 14, 2003
· Johnson, Caleb. "The Native Americans, Native Americans
   and the Plymouth Colony", Mayflower Web Pages;
   1997 and 1998
· Johnson, David. "The History of Martin Luther King Day
   and Martin Luther King Jr. Biography", Pearson
   Education; 2000-2003

· Keen, Judy. "White House Weighs Response to Kay", USA Today; January 30, 2004

· King, John and Suzanne Malveaux. "Bush: U.S. Will Move on Iraq if U.N. Won't", CNN; September 13, 2002

· Krane, Jim. "Clusters of Tents in Kuwait Serves as U.S. Military's Chief Mortuary For Iraq War", The Associated Press; February 21, 2004

· Levine, Art. "A New Bronze Age for the Tanning Industry", U.S. News & World Report; September 8, 1997

· Lyman, Brian. "Towns Join Indian Tax Suit", Norwich Bulletin; October 2, 2003

· MSN India. "Some U.S. POW's Identified"; March 24, 2003

· Marable, Manning. "Stealing The Election: The Compromises of 1876 and 2000"; December 2000

· Mikkelsen, Randall. "Bush Says Working to Overhaul Iraq Transition", Reuters; November 13, 2003

· Milbank, Dana. "Bush Disavows Hussein - Sept. 11 Link", Washington Post; September 18, 2003

· Moniz, Dave and Tom Squitieri, "After Grim Rumsfeld Memo, White House Supports Him", USA Today; October 22, 2003

· Moore, Michael. "Stupid White Men", Harper Collins Publishers Inc.; 2001

· Mount Vernon Ladies Association. "George Washington and Slavery", Mount Vernon Educational Resources; 2000

· NACS Online. "New York State Wants to Delay Fair Tax Collection 'Indefinitely'"; February 12, 2004

· NPR News. "Beyond The War in Iraq: Chronology", U.S. State Department; 2004

· Nash, Collin. "Nassau Rental Bias Reported", Newsday.com; February 12, 2004

· OnBaseMarketing.com. "Military Demographics"; 2004

· Palast, Gregory. "A Blacklist Burning For Bush", The Observer; December 10, 2000

· Palast, Gregory. "Florida's 'Disappeared Voters': Disenfranchised by the GOP", The Observer; February 5, 2001

· Parrish, Geov. "The Return of Dr. Martin Luther King, Jr.", Workingforchange.com; January 16, 2003

233

· People For The American Way. "Thanks Senators for
    Opposing Extremist Bush Nominees"; 2004
· Pfleger, Katherine. "Pre-War Intelligence on Iraq Was
    Flawed, Kay Testifies", The Associated Press;
    January 28, 2004
· Pitts, David and Thomas Eichler. "U.S. Supreme Court
    Decision Appears to Advance Bush Election Effort",
    U.S. Embassy; December 12, 2000
· Pressley, Sue Ann. "Bomb Kills Dozens in Oklahoma
    Federal Building", Washington Post; April 20, 1995
· Priest, Dana, William Booth, and Susan Schmidt. "Jessica
    Lynch Re-Visited: Interviews Add to Account of
    Capture, Rescue", Washington Post; June 19, 2003
· Reclaimamerica.org. "Judge Roy Moore News Story
    Timeline"; November 14, 2003
· Reuters. "U.S. Arms Inspector Resigns Iraq Had no
    WMD"; January 24, 2004
· Robinson, Susan. "Brown vs. Board of Education", Gibbs
    Magazine; Printed 2004
· Ryan, Joal. "Rush To Divorce - Again"; Eonline.com; June
    11, 2004
· Scheff, Liam. "Winning the Election - The Republican
    Way: Racism, Theft, and Fraud in Florida", The
    Observer; April 22, 2003
· School Net Network. "An Affair to Remember (Thomas
    Jefferson)"; March 2000
· Seneca Nation of Indians. "Honor Indian Treaties"
· Shifrell, Scott; Emily Gest and Greg Gittrich. "Five
    Officers Bodies, a Civilian Found in WTC Rubble",
    New York Daily News; February 10, 2002
· Slavin, Barbara. "U.S. Pushes the U.N. to Help With Iraq
    Exit", USA Today; January 20, 2004
· Sloan, Samuel. "The Slave Children of Thomas Jefferson",
    Kiseido Publishing; 1998
· Smith, Dennis. "Report From Ground Zero", Penguin
    Group; 2002
· Southern Poverty Law Center. "Monitoring Hate and
    Extremist Activity"; 2003

· Susskind, Ron. "The Price of Loyalty: George W. Bush,
The White House, and the Education of Paul
O'Neill", Simon & Schuster Adult Publishing; 2004
· Toobin, Jeffrey. "Too Close to Call: The Thirty-Six Day
Battle to Decide the 2000 Election", Random House
Publishing Group; 2002
· Thomas, Evan. "I Am Addicted to Prescription Pain
Medication", NEWSWEEK; October 20, 2003
· Tuchman, Gary and The Associated Press. "Civil Rights
Commission Opens Hearings on Florida Vote",
CNN; January 11, 2001
· Tuchman, Gary and The Associated Press. "Florida
Secretary of State Katherine Harris Defends Actions
in November Election", CNN; January 12, 2001
· USA Today. "Intelligence Lapses Corrupt Policy of Preemptive
Strikes"; January 30, 2004
· UseekUfind.com. "Bombing of the Sixteenth Street Baptist
Church"
· Von Drehle, David and R. Jeffrey Smith. "U.S. Strikes Iraq
for Plot to Kill Bush", Washington Post; June 27, 1993
· Weller, Robert. "Police Said Warning of Columbine
Killers", Associated Press; February 28, 2004
· WNDU-TV. "Civil Rights Commission Censures Florida
Election Procedures"; March 9, 2001
· WhiteHouse.gov. "Excerpts From the State of the Union
Regarding Iraq"; January 28, 2003
· Who2.com. "On the Money"; 2004
· Wikipedia. "Lori Piestewa"; August 2003
· Wikipedia. "Strom Thurmond"; February 2004
· Williams, Armstrong. "Was Abraham Lincoln a Friend to
Blacks? A View From the Right", Black
AmericaWeb News; February 16, 2004
· Winbush, Raymond. "Was Abraham Lincoln a Friend to
Blacks? A View From the Left", Black AmericaWeb
News; February 16, 2004
· Wingfield, Kyle. "Ten Commandments Judge Removed
From Bench", The Associated Press; November 14,
2003
· Woolls, Daniel. "Spanish Leader Pulls Troops From Iraq",
The Associated Press; April 18, 2004

· Yergin, Daniel. "The Prize", Simon & Schuster; 1991
· York, Byron. "The Cross Burning Case: What Really
      Happened", National Review; January 9, 2003
· Yost, Pete. "Bush Said Iraq Talks Concerned Afghanistan",
      The Associated Press; April 8, 2004
· Zarrella, John and Ian Christopher McCaleb. "Bush Still
      Wins Florida in Newspaper Recount", CNN; April 4, 2001

Proudly published by The Passion Profit Company
"Everyone has a passion. Every passion has value.
You CAN make money doing what you love!"

Learn how we can help you tell your own story at
www.passionprofit.com

Other books by the publisher:

The Passion Profit™ Series

The Hip Hop Entrepreneur™ Series

The Jamaican Nomad series

F. Sharp™ Observation series

The Ageless Adept™ Series

The Best of Saipan™ Series: